Public Relations for the Public Good

Public Relations for the Public Good

How PR has shaped America's Social Movements

Louis Capozzi
Shelley Spector

Public Relations for the Public Good: How PR has shaped America's Social Movements

First published in 2016 by
Business Expert Press, LLC
222 East 46th Street, New York, NY 10017
www.businessexpertpress.com

ISBN-13: 978-1-63157-381-1 (paperback)
ISBN-13: 978-1-63157-382-8 (e-book)

Business Expert Press Public Relations Collection

Collection ISSN: 2157-345X (print)
Collection ISSN: 2157-3476 (electronic)

Cover and interior design by S4Carlisle Publishing Services
Private Ltd., Chennai, India

First edition: 2016

10 9 8 7 6 5 4 3 2 1

Printed in the United States of America.

Abstract

While the profession of public relations is only a century old, man has been practicing the art of influencing public attitudes since the dawn of civilization. This book looks at modern America through the lens of public relations, showing how many of the events that have changed the course of our nation's modern history were triggered by campaigns to influence attitudes, opinions, and behaviors.

And while the channels may have evolved in the modern era—from radio and newspapers, billboards and magazine ads, to television and the Internet, to Tumblr and Instagram—the underlying power of public relations to shape organizations and issues, and to change human behavior has not.

Inside this book you'll find case studies on campaigns from the Women's Movement through Civil Rights to public education on health and safety issues that document the role public relations has played in shaping contemporary American culture and society.

Keywords

Activism, Awareness, Civil Rights, Communications, Democracy, Diversity, Equal justice, Gender equality, Influence, Influencers, Key audiences, Key publics, Labor, Media, Messaging, Outreach, Persuasion, Political Movements, Protests, Public Health Movements, Public opinion, Public Relations, Public Service, Publicity, Racial equality, Religious equality, Social Change, Social Movements, Strategy, Strategic Communications, Tactics, Women's Movements

Contents

Preface

By Harold Burson

There's a common misconception that public relations serves only commercial interests, mainly large corporations.

But looking back on the greatest social movements in American history, we learn that the most successful of them were achieved by passionate people who innately understood how to act and communicate in a manner that shaped public opinion and mobilized support for their causes.

Even though "public relations professionals" were not involved in many of these social upheavals—females seeking the right to vote, for example, or the abolition of slavery—their success depended on what we today would describe as the application of sound public relations principles. In effect, public relations is an applied social science that influences behavior which, when communicated effectively, motivates individuals or groups to a specific course of action by creating, changing, or reinforcing opinions and attitudes.

The stories presented in this book were powered by people who instinctively knew how to behave and communicate in a way that built support for their causes—using what today we would consider "best practices" in public relations.

The powers of strategic communications campaigns find their roots in insights about our audiences. We build on those insights to advise our clients on behavior that aligns them with the interests of those audiences, and we create campaigns that resound with them, moving them forward.

We, living in a democracy, have all been touched and affected by these campaigns—equal opportunity regardless of gender, race, religion, sexual orientation is a good relatively recent example. The campaigns have helped make us the most powerful nation in the world and the country that has attracted more immigrants for the better part of two centuries—where residents and institutions alike act on their conscience rather than solely on their self-interest.

Lou Capozzi and Shelley Spector have assembled a unique collection of the ways strategic communications campaigns have shaped America and worked for the public good. Their book should be a compelling read for students considering a career in our rapidly growing profession, and for all others seeking to understand "public relations" and the positive role it plays in society.

Harold Burson is the Founding Chairman of Burson-Marsteller, one of the world's leading public relations firms.

Introduction

What would the labor, safety, and temperance movements have in common with the founding of Israel? All of them were spurred by social change, grassroots fire, and belief in the cause. They were not what we would consider professional public relations programs in the literal sense. But their use of persuasive communications tactics and strategies were as powerful as any program run by a major firm or company today.

In recent years, more and more scholarship has developed around the influence of public relations on world history, especially with regard to social movements. This book explores the phenomenon through the lens of major contemporary social movements. It matters little whether the tools are using telegram or Instagram. It's the message—not the medium—that counts.

Readers will see that public relations is not only about promoting products, politics, and personalities. The profession has been the underlying force driving social change throughout history. By studying the campaigns, such as those included here, we can see some of the most genuine examples of consensus building and attitude change, and see how the power of public relations can work to make the world a better place.

These inspiring studies of social action—or public relations in history—are meant to give the reader both an opportunity to see public relations in a nonbusiness light, and to motivate those of us with an itch to make change to see how it's possible by using the most tools of public relations to spread the story.

The stories also show how the fervor of dedicated individuals—usually without a dime to spare—can light the fire under the public and set ablaze an entirely new set up of public attitudes for the public good.

Both Louis Capozzi and Shelley Spector teach in the master's program at Baruch College. Shelley, who has a passion for the history of our profession, was teaching a course on the subject and offered to engage her students in the project. Lou had taken a similar approach in a book on Crisis Management which included cases contributed by students. So

Shelley asked her students to contribute cases on subjects of their choice that showed the role public relations has played in shaping American culture and history.

Their case studies, along with chapters submitted by leading academics, are the foundation of this book. Thanks to everyone who contributed their case studies, which were edited and expanded by the authors.

Chapter 1: The Public Relations Campaign to Free Rosa Lee Ingram
Denise Hill, PhD
Assistant Professor of Strategic Communication
School of Communications, Elon University
Chapter 2: A Public Relations-Driven Evolution: Consumerism to Community Support
Anu Jagga-Narang
Chapter 3: Fostering a New Black Identity: The Harlem Renaissance Movement (1920–1939)
Kareem Scott Mumford
Chapter 4: Michael Sam Makes Great Gains for the LGBT Movement
Joseph Michael Cabosky, JD, PhD
Assistant Professor—Public Relations, Professional Track
School of Media and Journalism
University of North Carolina at Chapel Hill
Chapter 5: The War on Tobacco
Rebecca Carriero
Chapter 6: The Campaign for Tobacco-Free Kids
Edmund Balogun
Chapter 7: When Music is the Message: How Reggae Spread the Rastafarian Movement
Jodi-Ann Morris
Chapter 8: Battling the Tide of Public Opinion to Build Support for a Jewish State
Julia Shteyman
Chapter 9: Feminism from *The Feminine Mystique* to Lean In
Stephanie Wajntraub

Chapter 10: The American Civil Rights Movement: The Use of Contemporary Public Relations Techniques by Dr. Martin Luther King, Jr.

Sara Dyer

Chapter 11: The Triangle Shirtwaist Factory Fire and the Rise of the Labor Safety Movement

Khiara McMillin

Chapter 12: The Fight against Income Inequality: From Huey Long to Occupy Wall Street

Rosanna Plasencia

Chapter 13: Taking Depression Out of the Closet

Beth Chonoles

Chapter 14: The Temperance Movement

George Damalas

We sincerely hope this book will act as a strong motivator to attract leading students and career changers to the profession of public relations. According to Pew Research, young people today are "racially diverse, economically stressed, and politically liberal." In other words, perfect candidates for a fast-growing profession where they can work on programs that change the world!

Shelley Spector and Louis Capozzi
June, 2016

CHAPTER 1

The Public Relations Campaign to Free Rosa Lee Ingram

On a chilly November morning in 1947, near the small town of Ellaville, Georgia, about 115 miles south of Atlanta, John Stratford confronted Rosa Lee Ingram. Stratford and Ingram, who were both sharecroppers, had a long-standing feud about Ingram's livestock running over Stratford's fields (Shadron 1991, p. 30). That morning, Stratford threatened to kill the cattle if Ingram could not control them. Ingram and two of her sons began looking for the animals; however, nothing would appease Stratford that day. According to Mrs. Ingram, he came at her with a rifle. She struggled with Stratford and her sons came to her aid, wresting the gun from him and hitting him on the head. In the end, John Stratford lay dead in the road that led from his farm to the Ingram's.

Rosa Lee Ingram, a 44-year-old, recently widowed black mother of 14 children, two of whom had died in infancy, was arrested later that day along with two of her sons, and charged with the murder of John Stratford, a 64-year-old white man. After a one-day trial in January 1948, Ingram and her sons were convicted of Stratford's murder and sentenced to die.

Although virtually unknown today, the Ingram case attracted widespread attention at the time, especially among blacks (Martin 1985, p. 251). After the trial, the National Association for the Advancement of Colored People (NAACP) heard of the Ingram's dilemma and became involved, concentrating on legal means to free the Ingrams. Another organization, the Civil Rights Congress (CRC), also joined the fight to support the Ingrams. However, the CRC believed that purely legal efforts would never obtain justice for persecuted minorities without public awareness of the dilemmas they faced (Horne 1988, p. 19). Therefore, the CRC decided to concentrate its efforts on public relations.

In addition, a women-led, CRC-affiliated organization, the National Committee to Free the Ingram Family (NCFIF), which later became the Women's Committee for Equal Justice (WCEJ), worked tirelessly to maintain public awareness of the case in order to secure the Ingram's freedom.

Context

According to historian Gerald Horne (1985), "it is impossible to write the history of the civil rights movement without reference to CRC" (p. 19). However, historians have not devoted much attention to the organization, possibly because of its Communist affiliation and its short life. But to ignore the CRC is to overlook the organization's successes in furthering black civil rights and its use of public relations strategies. By examining the CRC's public relations efforts on behalf of Rosa Lee Ingram, the authors hope to bring attention to this overlooked but important organization. In addition, although a few studies of the CRC have reviewed the organization's tactics and strategies to create awareness, they have not done so through the lens of public relations.

Background

In the early part of the 20th century, the lynching of blacks by white southerners was a "reign of terror that was used to maintain the power whites had over blacks, a way to keep blacks fearful and to forestall black progress and miscegenation" (Dray 2002, p. xi). For decades, lynching was "an awesome destructive power, murderous to some, menacing to a great many, a constant source of intimidation to all black Southerners young and old and a daily reminder of their defenselessness." In addition, "legal lynchings," in which innocent black defendants were convicted of crimes and given sentences much harsher than white counterparts, reflected the power of the southern legal system to enforce codes of racial behavior and helped whites maintain their established social order (Rise 1992, p. 462). Although most of these legal lynchings involved black males, a variation from this pattern was the controversial murder prosecution of Rosa Lee

Ingram (Martin 1985). The Ingram case was one of the few that catapulted a female prisoner into prominence (Horn 1988).

About the CRC

Founded in Detroit in 1946, the CRC arose out of the merger of three groups with ties to the Communist Party USA: the International Labor Defense (ILD), the National Negro Congress, and the National Federation for Constitutional Liberties (Horne 1988). Embodying the spirit and tactics of all three of its predecessors, the CRC concentrated on legal defense, publicity, and mass political action on behalf of victims of illegal frame-ups. The CRC sought to protect the rights of labor and of racial, national, religious, and political minorities. It briefly became a major force in post-World War II civil rights battles for blacks, and for civil liberties for both white and black labor movement radicals, before becoming a victim of Cold War anticommunism and government repression (Martin 1987). Former ILD secretary William Patterson led the group throughout its existence.

The CRC provided assistance to individuals under investigation by the House Un-American Activities Committee, and in doing so became known as a Communist-affiliated organization. To counter this perception, the group began to give greater emphasis to black's legal rights and antidiscrimination activities. Major CRC campaigns on behalf of black defendants included the cases of Willie McGee, the Martinsville Seven, the Trenton Six, and Rosa Lee Ingram. CRC campaigns helped pioneer many of the tactics that Civil Rights Movement activists would employ in the late 1950s and 1960s (Horne 1988). Beyond this, the CRC was among the first organizations to expose American racism in the international arena and to connect it to U.S. Cold War foreign policy. In 1951, these efforts culminated in William Patterson's landmark study "We Charge Genocide," which he presented to the General Assembly of the United Nations. That study argued that the U.S. government was guilty of genocide under the UN Genocide Convention for its failure to act against lynching in the United States

By the mid-1950s, caught up in the United States' staunch anticommunism, the CRC was increasingly forced to defend its own members and affiliates against government prosecution. The financial strain of these efforts ultimately brought about the organization's dissolution in 1956.

Overview of the Rosa Lee Ingram Case

According to Rosa Lee Ingram and her sons, she had been threatened and sexually harassed by John Stratford. At their trial, Mrs. Ingram and her sons, Wallace, 16, and Sammie Lee, 14, all insisted that she had merely defended herself against an armed attack and the two teenagers had simply come to her aid. After they were arrested, the Ingrams were put in separate jails. They were not told they had the right to an attorney nor were they informed of their Fifth Amendment rights (Martin 1987, p. 36).

An all-white, all-male jury returned a murder conviction and sentenced the Ingrams to die in Georgia's electric chair. After news of the convictions and death sentences reached Atlanta and the North, a number of organizations came to the family's defense by raising money for them and sending telegrams to the judge presiding over the case. In February 1948, the NAACP received permission from the Ingram family to handle their defense, with NAACP Legal Defense Director Thurgood Marshall declaring that the fight to free the Ingrams had just begun (Martin 1987, p. 35).

Public Relations Plans, Strategies, Tactics to Free the Ingrams

As soon as the Ingrams were convicted, the black press began covering the story. *The Pittsburgh Courier* covered the case extensively, as did the *Chicago Defender*, the *Afro-American*, the *Atlanta Daily World*, the *Philadelphia Tribune*, the *New York Amsterdam News,* and *Jet* magazine. Although not as extensively, the local white press, including the *Ellaville Sun*, the *Atlanta Constitution,* and the *Americus Times-Recorder* also wrote about the case. A few stories also appeared in the *The New York Times* and *The Washington Post.* When the NAACP began providing legal counsel to the Ingrams in February 1948, the organization immediately requested a new trial. Due to public awareness of the case, funds for the family began pouring in and scores of letters and telegrams were sent to officials in Georgia from various parts of the country demanding a new trial (Shadron 1991).

Also, according to Martin (1987, p. 36), in February 1948, the CRC decided to adopt the case. The CRC began holding rallies in black churches in the North and wrote and distributed copies of a pamphlet about the case. The public pressure resulted in the Ingram's sentence being reduced from death to life in prison. They would be eligible for parole in seven years. In the meantime, the CRC, NAACP, and *Pittsburgh Courier* all mounted campaigns to raise additional funds for the Ingram family.

In July 1948, the Georgia Supreme Court upheld the Ingrams' convictions. As a result, the NAACP shifted its legal tactics to obtaining a pardon or parole through a behind-the-scenes approach to Georgia officials. The CRC did not agree with what it believed was a low-key method and instead believed that only maintaining public awareness and putting public pressure on Georgia officials would free the Ingrams. On the other hand, the NAACP felt that the CRC's tactics were overly flamboyant and aggressive and as such, would create additional hostility toward the Ingrams. Despite the conflict between the NAACP and the CRC, both organizations shared the same goal: to prevent the execution of the wrongly accused Ingram family, and then to secure their freedom.

While the fundraising for the Ingrams continued, the CRC turned planning and coordination of the Ingram campaign to the NCFIF, which was formed on March 21, 1949, "for the sole purpose of creating public sentiment and opinion on behalf of freedom for the Ingrams" (CRC papers, n.d., Reel 5, Box 8). The NCFIF further defined itself and its aim as "a nonpolitical, nonpartisan, interracial committee, organized for the sole purpose of securing unconditional freedom for Mrs. Rosa Lee Ingram and her two sons in Georgia, by arousing the conscience of America. Our aim is to exert moral pressure by every means available in order to wipe this horrible shame from America."

The NCFIF, comprised solely of women, included CRC and non-CRC members and was modeled after some of the earlier black women's clubs, which formally began in the late nineteenth century (Lerner 1974). According to McDuffie (2008) some members of the Sojourners for Truth and Justice, a black women's social protest organization, also joined the NCFIF. Mary Church Terrell, a prominent black civic leader and activist who had been a cofounder of the National Association of Colored Women, was named as national chairman of the Committee.

Early on the NCFIF developed a written plan, which they identified as "an outline for some actions and general program to start Ingram campaign" (CRC papers, n.d., Reel 5, Box 8). Their plan stressed not only the importance of black women's involvement, but also the need for the support of white women as noted in the discussion:

> The Ingram campaign can also provide white women with a unique opportunity to raise their level of responsibility to and participation in the fight against Jim Crow oppression. White women must fight boldly and uncompromisingly for the freedom of their Negro sisters in their own communities, organizations, churches, etc. (CRC papers, n.d., Reel 5, Box 8)

Also included in the outline under the heading "Public Relations, Publicity, Etc." was the following list ("Outline of Ingram Freedom Fight" n.d.):

> Foreign press, colonial press, etc.
> Material prepared for columnists on Negro and White press
> Special material to women's columnists
> Radio interviews
> Left press—March of Labor, Guardian, Masses & Mainstream, etc.
> Visits to various world organizations, letters, etc., to get Ingram case on agenda.
> Speakers Bureau
> Script—standard to be sent out when speakers unavailable

As a further testament to its planning and organization, the NCFIF prepared another outline of its activities. In an "Outline of Ingram Freedom Fight," the group identified its strategic aim as "freedom of Rosa Lee Ingram," with "exposure of the tactics of persecutors" ("Petition to President Truman" n.d.). Also included in the plan were tactical steps, such as sending delegations to the United Nations, and what the Committee referred to as "educational steps," listed as "new fact sheet (prepare at once); new pamphlet for united front, material suggested for parallel action and Ingram petition for Mother's Day."

In addition, the outline defined the campaign's basic slogans as "Free Rosa Lee Ingram," and "Racist Justice Must End." Part of the NCFIF's plan included "international solidarity actions," specifically "appeal to world federation of women," along with "parallel actions in U.S.A.," which included "all women's organizations to be reached" and "send out copies of action program." To maintain awareness, publicity was specified on the outline, with a focus on "newspapers—feature stories; magazines: *Ebony*, *Our World*, *Argosy*, etc.; and release: European, Asian, American."

One of the NCFIF's first activities was to send a delegation of northern women to visit Mrs. Ingram and check on her health. Shortly after the visit, prison officials moved Mrs. Ingram to another prison, complaining that ongoing visits, telegrams, and long-distance phone calls disrupted prison operations.

One of the Committee's primary audiences was women, and one of its strategies was to highlight two important gender-related issues: Mrs. Ingram was a mother, and she was a victim of male assault. In May 1949, the NCFIF sponsored Mother's Day rallies for Mrs. Ingram in black churches, which became an annual activity.

To further Mrs. Ingram's cause, the NCFIF launched a petition drive, eventually gathering 30,000 signatures that it delivered to the White House on June 1, 1949. Addressed to President Harry Truman, the petition stated that "it is a blot on the conscience of America that this woman should remain in prison because she dared to defend her children, her honor, her dignity and her life from the attacks of an enraged white farmer" ("Petition to President Truman" n.d.). Once again highlighting the collective appeal of women and motherhood, the petition urged the President to free Rosa Lee Ingram. "The American people, and particularly the mothers, implore you, Mr. President, to free Rosa Lee Ingram so she can be home with her children." When she presented the petitions, Mary Church Terrell gave a speech that noted it was "the duty of colored women to acquaint the citizens of this country with the details of this crime perpetrated upon an innocent, upright woman of their own group" (Terrell n.d.). However, she stressed that it was important that "women of all races, all creeds, and all nationalities" be aware of the case. Speaking to white women, she called for "the support and sympathy of many women of the dominant race who realize that by identifying themselves with this just cause they are assuring the protection of the women of all racial groups in the United States."

In September, the NCFIF asked W.E.B. Du Bois to draft a petition to the United Nations protesting Mrs. Ingram's sentence and the treatment of blacks in Georgia. The petition was presented to 59 UN delegates, with a request that they bring it to the floor of the General Assembly. This effort was part of the Committee's strategy to create international awareness of the Ingram's situation. As a result, the Ingram case received support from a number of international women's organizations ("Voices from Abroad" n.d.; "Women Around World Protest Ingram Imprisonment" 1949).

The following year, the Committee printed Mother's Day cards with Mrs. Ingram's picture. The cards were actually two cards printed on one piece of paper, to be cut into two cards and sent to two different locations. One card was addressed to Mrs. Ingram at Reidsville Prison in Reidsville, Georgia. The other card was addressed to Governor Herman Talmadge at the State Capitol, Atlanta Georgia. The wording on the card read as follows:

> Mrs. Rosa Lee Ingram, now 42, is a mother of fourteen children (two dead) and a widow since August, 1947, when her 64-year-old husband died. May 14, 1950 will be the third Mother's Day Mrs. Ingram has been in prison with her two young sons. This mother is in prison because she defended her honor and her home. The sons are in prison because they defended their mother.
>
> On Mother's Day—May 14, 1950—we honor and revere this widowed sharecropper and mother of fourteen children for her dignity and courage. Make 1950 Freedom Year for Mrs. Ingram and her two sons ("Mother's Day Card, 1950" n.d.).

In addition, the NCFIF printed and disseminated numerous brochures, flyers, fact sheets, pamphlets, and the occasional "Ingram Newsletter." One pamphlet featured "A Call to the Women of the United States" (CRC papers n.d., Reel 5, Box 8). As with most of the material produced, this document highlighted that Mrs. Ingram was "a woman, a Negro woman, mother of 14 children." Mrs. Ingram was also portrayed as a victim of racial and male oppression. She was "accosted by a white sharecropper," sentenced by "a white supremacist jury," and "Mrs. Ingram dared defend her dignity and honor against the attack of a white man." By focusing on gender, the Committee could also appeal to all women, not just black women. One such appeal on a fact sheet was:

> Negro women well know that their freedom is bound to the freedom of Rosa Lee Ingram. It is high time white women recognize that this holds just as true for them. For over 300 years, and particularly in the South, Negro men have been lynched and Negro people deprived of all rights under the false cry of "protecting white womanhood." White women can truly protect their rights only when they join with their Negro sisters to protect the rights of all women. ("Free Rosa Lee Ingram fact sheet" n.d.)

The wording on one flyer highlighted the racial injustice of the case, while calling on black and white women to work together: "People the world over know that Rosa Lee Ingram is imprisoned and hate the lynch law that jails her. Negro and white women, joining together to free Mrs. Ingram, take a great step toward winning the right of every human being to live in peace and freedom" ("Ingram Rally Invitation" n.d.).

The NCFIF later changed its name to the WCEJ to attract broader support. They sent invitations to churches, unions, and synagogues asking citizens to join a Mother's Day Crusade for Freedom. The invitation for one such Mother's Day event featured a photograph of two of Rosa Lee Ingram's children, along with Mrs. Ingram's own mother. The appeal was made from Mary Church Terrell, herself a mother, and included her photograph and signature. "Throughout our land sons and daughters of all colors and creeds will pay tribute to their mothers. Yet there are no sons who have honored their mother more than the sons of Rosa Lee Ingram" ("Ingram Rally Invitation" n.d.).

On April 13 and 14, 1950, the WCEJ held a rally in front of the United States delegation to the United Nations. The Committee had individuals dressed in historical costumes representing four famous activist women. In keeping with their strategy to involve both black and white women, the costumes showcased two black and two white female historical figures: Harriet Tubman, Sojourner Truth, Susan B. Anthony, and Elizabeth Cady Stanton. Among the slogans and signage used that day were "Proclaim Mother's Day as Freedom day for Mrs. Rosa Lee Ingram," "We fought for Woman's Suffrage and won," "We fought for Abolition of slavery and won," "We came back to free Mrs. Rosa Lee Ingram and her sons," "Human Rights means Freedom for Mrs. Ingram!" ("General Invitation Letter from Maude Katz" n.d.).

The WCEJ continued to hold rallies and prayer meetings; black and white women were invited to these events. To maintain awareness of the case, it also published and distributed educational material, which often included a direct call to action. For example, one fact sheet included four headings: The Stake of American Womanhood, The Stake of Labor, What Has Been Done, and What You Can Do. In the latter section, citizens were told, "you can help by sending letters and telegrams to Pres. Truman, asking that he use his good offices to secure for the Ingram family a full and unconditional pardon. You can also help the work of freeing this innocent mother and her sons by contributing funds to pay the expenses of a freedom campaign" ("The Facts of the Ingram Case pamphlet" n.d.). The fact sheet included a section that could be mailed to the WCEJ headquarters in New York, and the supporter could check three options indicating whether they had written or telegraphed President Truman urging a pardon; whether they would like to contribute and if so, the amount of their contribution; and whether they would like to order copies of the fact sheet at five cents each.

Another flyer the Committee prepared urged citizens to take the following action: "Write to President Truman to Free the Ingram Family now. Get your neighbor, friend, and organization to write to the President today. Urge your Minister, Congressman, Governor, Legislator, Mayor, and Councilman to do the same. Write to the Governor of Georgia" ("The United States Can Intervene for Human Rights flyer" n.d.).

On December 18, 1953, the WCEJ held a conference and prayer meeting in Atlanta. As part of its strategy, women's groups (regardless of race or religion) were invited to attend. One such group was the Emma Lazarus Federation of Jewish Women's Clubs, which affirmed its support of the Ingram case in a written statement. The Federation "agrees with Mrs. Mary Church Terrel [sic], Chairman of the Women's Committee for Equal Justice, that white women can truly protect their rights only when they join with their Negro sisters to protect the rights of all women" ("Statement from Emma Lazarus Federation of Jewish Women's Club for conference and holiday season prayer meeting for the Freedom of Mrs. Rosa Lee Ingram and her sons in Atlanta, Georgia, on Friday, December 18, 1953" n.d.). In its statement, the Lazarus Federation invoked the image of motherhood, reflecting one of the Committee's strategies. The Federation's executive director wrote, "as we lit the Chanukah candles this year, the image of this brave Negro mother merged for us with the image of the heroic Chanah, widowed mother of seven Jewish sons who refused to denounce her people. . . ." In addition, the Lazarus Federation sent a delegation to Atlanta, and it described the trip in the February 1954 issue of *Jewish Life*. Jennie Truchman (1954) a delegate who traveled from New York to Atlanta, wrote that "the thought that kept racing through my head was that as a Jewish woman I had a deep kinship with Mrs. Ingram, that I had a responsibility to help get her free" (p. 18). She added,

> We know that hatred against one group eventually means the effort to strangle others. The enemy of the Jew and the Negro is the same, though the Negro is far more intensely the object of that enmity. Jewish women have to take a stand to defend the democratic rights of the Negro people and especially of Negro women. It is time to end the 300-year-old story of the many Mrs. Ingrams." (p. 18)

To maintain public awareness and foster action to free the Ingrams, the WCEJ continued to hold Ingram rallies on Mother's Day, distribute press releases, send delegations to the Georgia State Capitol and take petitions to the U.S. Justice Department and the White House (Martin 1987). As a result, the black press kept the Ingram's story alive ("Family finally together again: Now the Ingrams have a home" 1960; "Atlanta nuptials: 'blue bloods' attend Ingram Son's Rites" 1960).

Further, according to Martin (1985) from a legal standpoint, "the case settled down to waiting for hearings by the Board of Pardons and Parole, which was not required by law to consider any parole requests by Mrs. Ingram prior to 1955, when she would have spent the minimum waiting period of seven years behind bars" (p. 265). "In February 1954, five months before her death at age 90, Mary Church Terrell led a group to Washington, D.C., or to meet with staff members of the U.S. Justice Department to press for a federal investigation. Also, a delegation presented a petition to the United Nations Commission on the Status of Women arguing that Rosa Lee Ingram's human rights had been violated. Meanwhile, prison officials continued to complain about the excessive letters and packages mailed to Mrs. Ingram, especially around Mother's Day" (p. 266).

In 1957, Georgia officials indicated they wished to be rid of the case, but the parole process continued for another two years (Martin 1985). On August 26, 1959, the Ingrams were finally freed after 12 years behind bars. According to Horne (1988, p. 207), they were freed because of the tireless and selfless efforts of the various groups and committees, specifically the mass pressure and public awareness campaigns. He argued that "the NAACP notwithstanding, the Ingram's prison tenure would have been even longer had it not been for this external pressure" (p. 212).

Evaluation

Assessing the effectiveness of the public relations strategies and tactics of the Ingram campaign should first involve a review of the Committee's (NCFIF and later WCEJ) objectives and goals. The overall objective was to free the Ingram family by arousing the conscience of America and exerting moral pressure by every means available. The CRC, the Committee to Free the Ingram Family, and the WCEJ developed and maintained a sustained campaign over time that achieved its goals. In addition, the Women's Committee had written plans with goals, strategies, audiences, and tactics.

The Committee employed the strategy of consistently and simultaneously employing multiple tactics and channels to achieve their aim. Rather than relying on a few tactics, the Committee used numerous print and face-to-face tools to engage in strategic two-way communication with their audiences. As part of its efforts to create awareness, the Committee defined what they wanted their audiences to know and what they wanted them to do. Their messages focused on facts of the Ingram case, the unjust incarceration, Mrs. Ingram's victimization, her race, her gender, and her motherhood. The Committees were also very specific in articulating the action they wanted their audiences to take, from asking supporters to sign a petition, attend a rally, provide financial support, or send a letter to Georgia Governor Talmadge or President Truman.

In analyzing the Committee's audiences, they targeted state and national officials; government organizations, such as the U.S. Justice Department; churches; unions; civic groups; women and women's clubs; international groups; the news media; the President of the United States, and very broadly, the American public. With some of these stakeholder groups (or audiences in nonpublic relations talk), the Committees were focused on educating and garnering support, sympathy, and engagement, while encouraging specific actions. With other stakeholders, the primary focus was on getting the specific audiences to take a particular action, for example, asking officials to open a federal investigation into the case.

Furthermore, the Committees recognized that women, especially mothers, were a primary stakeholder. Capitalizing on their previous experience with the black women's club movement, members of the Committees were able to use motherhood and gender as a common link shared by all women, regardless of race. As Lerner (1974, p. 1959) notes, black and white women had a long history of forming clubs to help bring about social reform. The need to organize such clubs often arose wherever a social need remained unmet. By the time Mary Church Terrell became involved with the campaign to free Rosa Lee Ingram, she had been a leader in the black women's club movement for most of her life (Sanderson 1973, p. 20). Often underscoring the work of black women in the club movement was the concept of motherhood and community mothering (Edwards 2000, p. 89). In doing so on behalf of Rosa Lee Ingram, they were able to engage and enlist the support of women across racial lines and geographies, even receiving support from women's groups internationally, who wrote letters to President Truman decrying Mrs. Ingram's imprisonment. Some of the media coverage highlighted that black and white women were working together on this cause (e.g., "Ingram Plea Renewed: 50 Whites and Negroes Urge Georgia Women's Release" 1954).

A Women's Cause

The efforts to free Rosa Lee Ingram truly reflected a public relations campaign developed by women, it targeted women, and its goal involved a woman. Members of the NCFIF and WCEJ committees often articulated their demands in maternal terms. In the material produced by the Committee, Rosa Lee Ingram was always described as a mother, specifically a doomed mother to 12 children.

In calling for her freedom, the messages in many of the Committees' materials focused on reuniting Rosa Lee Ingram with her children. In addition, she was identified as a widow, and as a woman who defended her honor from a white male attacker. Furthermore, the Ingram Committee charged that her unjust conviction was "an outrage to all American motherhood and womanhood" ("If you would be free, free Rosa Lee Ingram" flyer n.d.). Because of the Committee's focus on motherhood, most of the news articles also focused on Rosa Lee Ingram as a woman and mother, as evidenced by headlines such as "Philadelphians rally to save doomed mother and two sons" ("Philadelphians Rally to Save Doomed Mother and 2 Sons" 1948) and "Mrs. Ingram's 10 Children Miss Mother" ("Mrs. Ingram's 10 Children Miss Mother" 1950).

The Committees also focused on gender by highlighting the problem of sexual violence committed against black women by white men. Rosa Lee Ingram fought for "her honor and dignity" ("Statement from Emma Lazarus Federation of Jewish Women's Club for conference and holiday season prayer meeting for the Freedom of Mrs. Rosa Lee Ingram and her sons in Atlanta, Georgia, on Friday, December 18, 1953" n.d.). The *Pittsburgh Courier* ("He Even Tried to Go With Me" 1948) even visualized the altercation between Mrs. Ingram and John Stratford by including three illustrations with one of its cover stories about the case. In one of the illustrations, Stratford was shown inviting Mrs. Ingram to go with him, presumably to assault her. In the next illustration, he is attacking Mrs. Ingram and in the final illustration, Stratford is being attacked by one of Mrs. Ingram's sons, with Mrs. Ingram seen in the background covering her eyes.

Not only did the Committee succeed in maintaining awareness of the Ingram case over a long time period, it used womanhood and motherhood as a strategy to gain moral support and engage a broader audience of women, both black and white.

Conclusion

Although rarely mentioned as part of the postwar black freedom movement, Rosa Lee Ingram was a household name in African American communities during her incarceration, and there was awareness of the case internationally. Black women took the lead in building the campaign to free Rosa Lee Ingram. Although these women would not be defined then as formal public relations practitioners, their work can be certainly considered public relations in the modern context.

In their focus on developing mutually beneficial relationships with their publics, the activists working on behalf of Rosa Lee Ingram followed the structure of a modern public relations campaign. They successfully articulated their goals, defined their audiences, and developed strategies and tactics, which they sustained over time to influence their constituents, thereby achieving their goals. They recognized the importance of public relations in their planning process, and many of the strategies and tactics they employed are those used by today's public relations professionals.

As a result of the tireless work and the public relations activities of the women in the Ingram committees, along with the support of the CRC and the legal work of the NAACP, Rosa Lee Ingram and her two sons were finally freed. Although it took 12 years, the organizations working on behalf of the Ingrams achieved their goal. Rosa Lee Ingram would go on to live another 21 years, dying peacefully on August 4, 1980 in Atlanta, Georgia.

Takeaway

This story, like many in the Civil Rights Movement, offers an excellent example of public relations as an engine for social change. The WCEJ used all the tools in the public relations toolbox—strategic planning, message development, media relations, special events (rallies), and public education materials (Mother's Day cards, newsletters, etc.).

Of note in this case is how well the Committee understood its constituencies, and how best to appeal to them. Rather than position this as a case of *racial* injustice, the Committee presented it as a case of *gender* injustice. By focusing on "motherhood," its messages could resonate with everyone, regardless of race, class, or gender. Thus, its tie-in with Mother's Day was particularly strategic, and newsworthy. Further broadening its appeal, the Committee worked closely with women's groups outside the African American Committee, such as the Emma Lazarus Federation of Jewish Women's Organizations. Such groups, which themselves had been fighting against inequality, provided the cause with "third-party" credibility, as well as a way to reach audiences that might otherwise not relate to the cause of a poor black woman.

With a formal plan, clear objectives, smart strategies, and effective tactics, the Committee produced a measureable result—freedom for the Ingram family.

CHAPTER 2

A Public Relations-Driven Evolution

Consumerism to Community Support

"Consumerism" has been, in some circles, a dirty word. A one-dimensional definition of the subject implies that people spend a lot of money on goods that do not provide any lasting satisfaction or happiness (Heath 2001). In today's society, this definition labels "consumerism" negatively because people's purchasing behavior presumably defines their self-identity; (1) planned and perceived obsolescence leads people to replace goods before needed (Utaka 2006); (2) consumerism leads to wasteful spending (Tilman 1999).

The negative label extends to the communications business as well. It implies that marketers and their communicators can manipulate the public into wanting and buying things they do not need and/or paying high prices for things made to seem more desirable by the communications.

To balance the scale, other dimensions of consumerism must be studied. The synergy between mass production and mass consumption of products and services that forms the basis of a strong economy is also an element of consumerism (Chase 1991). This aspect of consumerism increases industrialization, creates jobs, and stimulates the economy.

The term *consumerism* first emerged in the late 17th century and grew during the 18th century in Western Europe describing an attraction for material goods (Trentmann 2004). The Industrial revolution in the mid-18th century revolutionized the way products were made and created millions of new jobs. Marketing communications—advertising and public relations—in the 18th century played a major role in creating an emphasis on fashion and increasing consumption of clothes, furniture, houses, and leisure (Brewer and Porter 2004, p. 208). The luxurious lives of aristocrats with power and excessive wealth allowed them to elaborate their material possessions in architecture, bodily adornment, and clothing (Stearns 2006). This display of wealth was well publicized in the media at the time, creating a desire to emulate the upper classes. Critics like Nigel Whiteley (1987) argued that the irrational desire to own goods in order to emulate those of higher social ranks contrasts with the political and economic necessity for growth. But others defended the campaigns as economically positive for society.

Consumerism migrated to the United States and became a hallmark of American society. Some social scientists and economists saw the shift in culture of "conspicuous consumption" (Veblen 2010) as immoral, asserting that the irrational behavior and mass production would hurt the environment and traditional values. Such media coverage as the editorial cartoon that appears later in this chapter portrayed consumers as greedy and irrational.

Others supported consumption as a virtue that gave people freedom to buy goods that made them happy (Stearns 1997). This view resounded with the public, and the personal lives of Americans were deeply affected by the shift in values redefining fulfillment.

Factors Driving Growth in Consumption

World War II became the first important influence driving the growth in consumption in the United States. The war cost the country $300 billion—equivalent to $4 trillion today ("War Bonds for the War Effort" n.d.). To help fund the effort, the government used public relations techniques to encourage Americans to invest in War Bonds, which would pay for the tanks, planes, uniforms, food, medicine etc. ("The U.S. Home Front at a Glance" n.d.). America was spending heavily on warfare while at the same time rationing consumer goods, which created shortages of many products. Manufacturers were forced to focus on war production, and Americans were encouraged to ration food and plant backyard "Victory Gardens" (see Figure 2.1). Government regulated the economy to control production, prices, and wages. Women joined the work force, both on the home front and battlefield. After men returned

Figure 2.1 Image Caption: Victory Gardens ("Victory Gardens during World War II" n.d.) *Courtesy: Farming in the 1940s*

from the war, women were forced to quit, although many of them wanted to retain their jobs ("Women in WWII at a Glance" n.d.).

Posters, advertisements, and public relations, and the government policies they reflected, shaped consumption in America during the war years. They also created a built-up demand for consumption that would be satisfied after the war.

In 1945, as the war ended and soldiers returned home, the American economy soared and consumer demand increased with it. People were eager to spend money on new, once-rationed, products, such as, nylon, Styrofoam, and plastics ("1940s War, Cold War and Consumerism" 2005). Fueled by politicians' rhetoric and other communications, Americans saw consumption as a patriotic activity that made the 1950s a decade of economic boom (Hart-Davis 2015). The post-World War II era, also known as the Golden Age of Capitalism, witnessed an abundance in the production of cars, televisions, and other consumer goods. The automobile, aviation, and electronics industries resumed production and grew exponentially (Veblen 2010). The development of malls and department stores dominated the consumer values in American economy and culture.

The boom in the fast food restaurant industry changed the eating habits of the people (Neuhaus 1999). The American economic system of scarcity and need changed to abundance and desire (Veblen 2010).

Following the war, defense spending and foreign aid stimulated the demand for American products in war-stricken countries, which further advanced the U.S. economy (Roark *et. al.* 2011). Jobs grew in the service sector and people gained more purchasing power. The high-consumption economy meant high-production market. The American economic system became highly dependent on mass consumption as the means of creating growth (Veblen 2010). From 1950 to 1965, wages doubled or tripled (Ryan 2011), increasing Americans' disposable income and purchasing power.

The government followed Keynesian principles of macroeconomic management (Logemann 2008), and promoted consumer society to level the playing field—prosperity for all instead of choice and luxury for few (Hilton 2007). Consumption was encouraged by using a wide range of public relations techniques and government policies as a path forward for all, rich and poor alike, with the promise of a higher standard of living. Enacted in 1944, the Servicemen's Readjustment Act (GI Bill of Rights) helped 16 million veterans with job training and education, unemployment compensation, and low-interest loans to pay for the house, farms, and small businesses (Ryan 2011), which further boosted the economy. All of these programs were actively supported with public relations campaigns.

From 1950 to 1960, newly married veterans moved out to the suburbs (Veblen 2010) in the pursuit of the "American dream" (Brohl 2001). The "baby boom" fueled a housing boom ("History: 1950s" 2003, September 13). The new suburbs were homogenous in race and class, with a relatively equal income group. Material possessions represented the social status and prestige (Veblen 2010). People accumulated those possessions in the form of cars, television, household appliances, baby goods, and leisurely dining in restaurants. Throughout the 1950s, 59 percent of American families owned at least one car ("History: 1950s" 2003, September 13).

Expansion of credit financing became another important element driving mass consumption. Credit financing democratized access to consumer goods, as many Americans presumed credit to be the road to the American Dream (Logemann 2008). Domestic purchasing power began to expand as Americans gained access to installment credit (Logemann 2008) to purchase items such as refrigerators, cars, and televisions. The introduction of the Diners Club and American Express credit cards made "buy now, pay later" mentality popular among the American middle class (Zumello 2011). Credit cards were promoted through major communication campaigns as a way to easily purchase consumer goods, so much so that from 1956 to 1967 the consumer debt increased by 133 percent (from $42.5 billion to $99.1 billion), and the credit card debt increased by 146 percent (from $31.7 billion to $77.6 billion). According to the Federal Reserve, the total outstanding consumer debt, not including mortgages, was $3.34 trillion as of February 2015, and the total credit card debt in America was $884.8 billion in January 2015.

The Critics

The controversy about "consumerism" as an issue was further fueled in the 1950s by Vance Packard's *The Hidden Persuaders* (1957, McKay), as well as by consumer advocate, corporate critic, and former presidential candidate, Ralph Nader. Packard's claim that advertising might affect people on a subliminal level sparked a public debate. Advertising and public relations executives on Madison Avenue were seen by many as inherently manipulative and dishonest. Many critics of consumerism believed that advertising, public relations, and media influence artificially created a modern society, rather than arising from people's needs and desires (Cain 2009).

In response to these critics, marketing, and public relations leaders emphasized their role as strategic management counselors, advising clients on both behavior and communication. Public relations pioneer Harold Burson, founder of Burson-Marsteller, the firm that bears his name, describes the function this way:

> The power of strategic communications finds its roots in insights about attitudes, opinions and behavior. We build on those insights to advise our clients on behavior that aligns them with the interests of their constituencies, and we create campaigns that resound with those audiences, moving them forward (Bates 2006).

The principles of public relations are also summed up in the words of Arthur Page, an early leader of communications at AT&T.

> All business in a democratic country begins with public permission and exists by public approval. If that be true, it follows that business should be cheerfully willing to tell the public what its policies are, what it is doing, and what it hopes to do. This seems practically a duty. (Cutlip n.d.)

Nader's consumer protection activities depict a dramatic vision of corporate greed that has compelled some consumer advocates and federal regulators to protect helpless consumers (Sowell 2004). Consumer protection, however, does not come free. The added cost to the consumers and deprivation of choice is the price consumers' pay (Brunk 1973). The economic growth post-World War II changed the seller's market to the buyer's market (Buskirk and Rothe 1970), giving consumers more power and understanding to buy products they wanted, when they wanted.

The Rise of Modern Marketing Communications

But one factor, above all others, influenced the shift in American attitudes toward consumption—TV commercials. With the advent of television came a new generation of sophisticated communicators, who used research-based insights to develop campaigns that would drive consumers to action.

The effort started even before the war ended. Marketers popularized the idea of "World of tomorrow" at the 1939 New York World's Fair, with massive advertising and public relations campaigns ("1940s War, Cold War and Consumerism" 2005). The campaigns created a sensation by portraying all the stylish, modern, and time-saving products that consumers will be able to purchase after the war was over.

As expected, Americans rushed to buy the products that were promoted soon after the war ended. Pent-up demand fueled a steady growth in manufacturing of consumer goods, which, in turn, created more jobs, and eventually increased consumer purchasing power.

The increase in mass consumption is also attributed to marketing communication campaigns which publicized the "American dream," depicting happy and healthy families, with usually two or three kids, alongside a shiny car or television ("The American Dream of the 1940s & 1950s" 2013). Manufacturers invested in new technologies to improve their products and seem more attractive than their competitors. The technological innovations of wartime were converted into labor saving convenience products ("History: 1950s" 2003, September 13). Television was the most influential innovation of the 1950s and advertising and promotion on TV proved to be a dominant medium. Cutting-edge communications strategies, such as motivational research, were used to portray a society with traditional American values combined with upward mobility and prosperity. The advertising industry also saw an increase in spending from $2.1billion in 1941 to $2.8 billion in 1945 to $5.7 billion in 1950 ("The American Dream of the 1940s & 1950s" 2013). The TV advertising spending saw a significant increase from $12.3 million in 1949 to $128 million in 1951 ("History: 1950s" 2003, September 13).

Television is ubiquitous in the American culture even in today's social media world. The number of households with at least one TV set grew from 1 million to 44 million from 1949 to 1969 ("Television during the 1950s and 60s" n.d.). Common national coverage of presidential elections and sports events connected America from coast to coast and generated a national dialogue. In 1952, TV advertising also revolutionized the presidential election contest between Dwight D. Eisenhower and Adlai E. Stevenson, providing Gen. Eisenhower an avenue to address the American people with pre-recorded messages. By 1960, TV reached 90 percent household penetration ("History: 1950s" 2003, September 13).

TV is a business—one that relies on advertising for its revenues. So, the main goal of television programming was to build an audience for the product advertisements (Allen and Coltrane 1966). Commercial advertising had a profound effect on American society and consumer culture. Advertisers and marketers bought time on television to advertise their products and services. Consumers were able to see the demonstration of products and how they functioned in the commercials. Television overcame the limitation of both print and radio ads. In the 1930s, radio "soap operas"—serialized dramas first sponsored by detergent producer Proctor & Gamble—were used to captivate housewives. At their peak, the radio "soaps" controlled 90 percent of all commercially sponsored daytime radio broadcast hours ("Encyclopedia of Television—Soap Opera" n.d.).

The first daytime TV soap opera in America was *These Are My Children* in 1949. The concept of soap operas transferred easily to television and managed to seize a loyal women viewership on a daily basis. Men, women, and children were presented in contrasting settings, performing different actions, and portraying various roles ("Misc 1950s Commercials [Part 11]" 2014; Allan and Coltrane, 1966). The advertising industry captured the attention of women through the daytime commercials in order to influence them to buy products by carefully crafted messages ("1950s TV Ad Ford Car" 2008, February 20). The messaging was mostly geared toward women—with tips of making their husbands happy by serving good coffee or doing laundry ("Folgers Coffee (1950s)—Classic TV Commercial" 2012; "1950s Laundry Detergent Commercial" 2012). Women were the managers of the household and responsible for 80 to 90 percent of consumption.

The direct correlation between advertising spending and personal spending is difficult to establish because of other factors such as demand, economy, and unemployment rate (Jacobson and Nicosia 1981). However, preliminary research suggests the presence of a causal relationship between advertising and consumption behavior over time (Young and Young 2004). By the end of 1950s, the United States had 6 percent of the world's population, consumed one-third of all the world's products and services, and made two-thirds of manufactured goods (Hart-Davis 2015).

Along with advertising, public relations field enjoyed immense popularity in the 1950s (Young and Young 2004). According to Bates (2006) "image advertising" promoted the corporate identity along with the products and services offered by the companies. Big corporations, such as AT&T, General Motors, General Electric, Standard Oil, Ford Motor Company, and many others sponsored programs such as *General Electric Theater* (1953–1962), to represent the companies in a positive light. After World War II, Bates (2006) noted that public relations became a popular means for government, corporations, and non-for-profit organizations to publicize their products and services in the prospering consumer markets.

Public Accountability

As communications evolved and matured, public relations and public accountability became a much greater factor in both corporate and marketing communications. In his book *Public Relations*, Edward Bernays (1952), a public relations pioneer, explained,

> The three main elements of public relations are practically as old as society: informing people, persuading people, or integrating people with people. Of course, the means and methods of accomplishing these ends have changed as society as changed.

Many historians of consumerism have cautioned against manipulation of consumers' subconscious desires by marketers and manufacturers. Manufacturers had to generate greater interest in consumption, and public relations and advertising played a major role. Marketers had to understand consumers to be able to successfully pitch the products for sale and create demand ("War Bonds for the War Effort" n.d.).

Public relations professionals define their role as influencing both organizational behavior and communications. Edward Bernays (1952), in *Public Relations*, described the profession as "a management function, which tabulates public attitudes, defines the policies, procedures, and interests of an organization . . . followed by executing a program of action to earn public understanding and acceptance."

Today, the Arthur Page Society, whose members include the leaders of corporate communications and major agencies, focuses strongly on the notion of public accountability. Its statement of principles (www.awpagesociety.com/site/the-page-principles) says,

1. *Tell the truth.* Let the public know what's happening and provide an accurate picture of the company's character, ideals, and practices.
2. *Prove it with action.* Public perception of an organization is determined 90 percent by what it does and 10 percent by what it says.
3. *Listen to the customer.* To serve the company well, understand what the public wants and needs. Keep top decision makers and other employees informed about public reaction to company products, policies, and practices.

4. *Manage for tomorrow.* Anticipate public reaction and eliminate practices that create difficulties. Generate goodwill.
5. *Conduct public relations as if the whole company depends on it.* Corporate relations are a management function. No corporate strategy should be implemented without considering its impact on the public. The public relations professional is a policymaker capable of handling a wide range of corporate communications activities.
6. *Realize a company's true character is expressed by its people.* The strongest opinions—good or bad—about a company are shaped by the words and deeds of its employees. As a result, every employee—active or retired—is involved with public relations. It is the responsibility of corporate communications to support each employee's capability and desire to be an honest, knowledgeable ambassador to customers, friends, shareowners, and public officials.
7. *Remain calm, patient, and good-humored.* Lay the groundwork for public relations miracles with consistent and reasoned attention to information and contacts. This may be difficult with today's contentious 24-hour news cycles and endless number of watchdog organizations. But when a crisis arises, remember, cool heads communicate best.

With the emergence of social media and the concepts of citizen journalists, public relations professionals have taken a lead role in shaping organizational behavior and communications.

A New Generation of Consumers

Millennials, born between early 1980s and early 2000s, represent a key consumer demographic of today and the future. In the United States, the Millennials account for a fourth of the population (Schawbel 2015) and an estimated $1.6 trillion in direct annual spending (Barton, Koslow, and Beauchamp 2015). Millennials are highly educated and career oriented. The leaders of future consumer behavior, Millennials develop brand loyalty for the companies that present quality products and are engaging on a personal and emotional level (Barton, Koslow, and Beauchamp 2015; Schawbel 2015). This "reciprocity principle" (Schawbel 2015) combined with the Internet, social media, and mobile devices have magnified the

Millennials' impact on how a company conducts business and which narrative drives the public opinion. The brand loyalty and spending behavior of Millennials is evident with recent research—only one percent of Millennials would trust a brand based on compelling advertising (Barton, Koslow, and Beauchamp 2015); however, 75 percent love brands that support local communities (Schawbel, 2015).

Strategic philanthropy is a public relations approach used by profit-making companies today to support causes that directly benefit the local or international communities, and simultaneously support the company's core business objectives (Parsons 2004). A well-executed strategic philanthropic public relations program integrates the needs of the cause or issue with the business objectives, creating a win–win situation for both ("What Is Strategic Philanthropy?" 2013).

According to Jerry Marx (1988 p. 31), "The aim of corporate philanthropy is to do well by doing good, and American corporations recognize their role and responsibility in solving social issues." Strategic philanthropy benefits the corporations in many ways (Marx 1988). First, the corporations are able to better control and evaluate the impact of charitable giving programs on business objectives and needs of a community. Second, the corporations enhance their public relations reach with the charities that get the contributions. And finally, strategic philanthropy improves employee motivation, productivity, and loyalty.

Procter & Gamble (P&G), a company that owns many popular consumer products that are pervasive in an American household, continues to contribute to society through strategic public relations programs (Kaufman n.d.). The company invests $2 billion annually on consumer research to ensure that its product innovations are consumer centric (Confino 2012). P&G sponsors over 15,000 research studies, with products that cover 5 million consumers in over 100 countries, and spends $350 million each year on in-home consumer research (Kaufman n.d.).

P&G has demonstrated noteworthy examples of strategic public relations by providing brand-specific help in the times of disaster. P&G's "Dawn Saves Wildlife" is one of the world's most recognized disaster relief effort ("Dawn Saves Wildlife—You Can Make A Difference With Dawn" n.d.). The Dawn dishwashing liquid has been used to rescue, clean, and release more than 75,000 animals affected by oil pollution from the 1989

Exxon Valdez oil spill and 2010 BP oil spill ("Companies in Action: Case Studies in Effective Corporate Disaster Relief" 2013). Similarly, "Tide loads of hope" is another disaster relief effort sponsored by P&G that provides mobile Laundromat, washing, drying, and folding clothes for families in need ("About—Loads of Hope" n.d.). From Louisiana after Hurricane Katrina to California after forest fires, the program has cleaned over 58,000 loads of laundry in communities without electricity or access to clean water (Steve 2009).

Chipotle's "Food with Integrity" is another example of a strategic program that integrates business objectives with community welfare. Food with Integrity is based on the principle of using locally grown ingredients that are free of genetically modified organisms (GMOs) and meats that come from sustainably raised animals ("Chipotle" n.d.). Chipotle Cultivate Foundation focuses on key food issues to support farmers, increase animal welfare, and reduce obesity in children. The "Cultivate a Better World" integrated marketing campaign highlights Chipotle as a global leader on these food issues, creates a strong awareness and emotionally connects with the consumers (Baylis 2012).

Conclusion

The practice of public relations today, often misrepresented as "publicity," integrates the communication and relationship between a company and its employees, suppliers, legislators, consumers, and community. These examples of public relations campaigns not only prove successful in giving back to the community and connect with consumers, but also help cultivate goodwill and profits for the corporations. Sales results for the P&G's public relations campaigns are confidential, but the company tracks marketing spending closely to business results, and one can assume that if they did not drive sales they would not be continued.

Consumer marketing communications, specifically public relations, has been instrumental in changing business practices, where companies today strive to shape the world for the better and simultaneously profit from the initiatives. Consumers are key stakeholders who buy from companies that share their view and values. As a result, companies have realized the need to nourish trustworthy relationships with consumers.

Based on what we know about the evolution of a consumer society and consumer behavior, and how public relations is instrumental in shaping attitudes of the corporations, the question "Is consumerism good or bad?" is easy to answer in the affirmative.

Takeaway

The dramatic power of communications was widely demonstrated with the rise of television and TV advertising. The public's concern about communications being used as a tool by big companies and their communicators to manipulate public opinion and behavior seems now, in hindsight, to have been inevitable.

Happily, in the ensuing 60 years, and especially the last decade, most corporations have learned the critical importance of aligning their behavior, and their communications, with the best interests of their constituencies. The growing role of the corporate communications officer has brought about a new era of corporate accountability, one that would frown upon the marketing tactics employed in the 1950s.

By aligning corporate and brand behavior with causes and ideas that audiences can connect with, today's sophisticated organizations are building credibility, trust, and brand value. The result has been a dramatic decline in the kinds of concerns "consumerists" raised in the postwar era.

So Arthur Page was right: All business in a democratic country *does* begin with public permission and exists by public approval.

CHAPTER 3

Fostering a New Black Identity

The Harlem Renaissance Movement (1920–1939)

The Harlem Renaissance used the power of public relations to foster the renewal and celebration of a new image for black Americans. The movement gave a voice and identity to a group of people who had been oppressed in the United States since the country's founding. Through literature, music, and art, the Harlem Renaissance became a symbol of progress and hope for black Americans, while addressing many of the political and social issues they faced. This movement is a quintessential example of how a social movement, fueled by the power of public relations, can change the attitudes of millions.

History

The movement emerged with the "Great Migration," which began shortly after World War I and ended in 1920. An estimated 1.5 million black Americans moved from the rural South to metropolitan cities in the North and Midwest to escape the Jim Crow segregation in the South and to create a better life (see Table 3.1) (Lewis 1987). Throughout the South, churches, barbershops, and local grocery stores had for years served as informal meeting places to keep up with community news. But in the early 1920s, with racial tensions brewing around them, these places were starting to serve a more crucial purpose: how to get out of town and move

Table 3.1 Population statistics for 1930

1930	Black population	Percentage (%) of Total population
New York	328,000	4.7
Chicago	234,000	6.9
Cleveland	72,000	8.0
Detroit	120,000	7.7
Philadelphia	220,000	11.3
Pittsburg	55,000	8.2
St. Louis	93,500	11.4

Source: Great Migration Interactive Map: MoMA. Campbell Gibson and Kay Jung. Population Division Working Paper—Historical Census Statistics on Population Totals By Race, 1790 to 1990, and By Hispanic Origin, 1970 to 1990. U.S. Census Bureau Working Paper Number 76, February 2005 (http://www.moma.org/interactives/exhibitions/2015/onewayticket/visualizing-the-great-migration/)

up to the "economic boom towns" in the North. The communities created "migration clubs" to help relocate families to New York, Chicago, Boston, and other cities (Trotter 1991). The migration clubs served as reliable trustworthy news sources for families looking to relocate, and word-of-mouth spread updates quickly. In today's public relations terms, these clubs would be called *advocacy groups*.

With a fair percentage of the black populations illiterate, verbal communications were the primary means of connecting, even though most yearned to get an education (Cornelius 1983). And, thanks to the Great Migration, most did.

Originally known as the "New Negro Movement," the 1920s Harlem Renaissance became a cultural force that fostered a new identity for black Americans. The movement began to transform the nation's perception of blacks from uneducated, impoverished former slaves to educated, artistic, and culturally conscious people. Yet, even in the 1920s North, racism still prevailed and economic opportunities for blacks were sparse. Nonetheless, talented blacks saw the artistic fields wide open to them as never before: publishing, art, theatre, recording, and film. A burgeoning entertainment business in the rich Roaring Twenties—with the advent of film "talkies," music recordings, burlesque, and Broadway—opened the doors to hundreds of black artists, whose appeal extended far beyond the black communities.

Philosopher and intellectual, Alain Locke, became one of the most outspoken leaders of the New Negro Movement (Williams 2010). As the first black American Rhodes Scholar, Locke's high level of education and trips abroad helped to build a new identity for the American black in cities overseas. Locke became an informal spokesperson for the movement and was credited as the "Father of the Harlem Renaissance" for his publication of *The New Negro* (1925)—a collection of poems and essays that elucidated the evolution of black Americans (Williams 2010). Locke resolved to remove the disparaging images and stereotypes of the "old Negro" through a "renewed self-respect and self-dependency" (Sellers 2014). This change would happen, he wrote, through ideas, art, literature, and music. "The New Negro Movement" caused a cultural shift that extended way beyond Harlem. Writers like Locke did much to erase the stereotypes of the old Negro.

Writers and Authors

The Harlem Renaissance sparked the first literary movement in black American history. Among the most influential writers were Claude McKay, Langston Hughes, Countee Cullen, Wallace Thurman, Jean Toomer, and Zora Neale Hurston. Many of them were well aware their literary works would have major impact on the public's perception of black Americans. They built a community of poets, critics, patrons, sponsors, and publishers which shared a common endeavor—to create a new awakening and pride in the heritage of the black American (Wintz 2013, p. 8).

Through their poetry, essays, memoirs, and novels, and their personal visibility through speeches, readings, and participation in events, these writers managed to paint a picture of the black experience in a way that had never been before. No doubt, many of these works proved to have considerable impact on the way white readers were now able to understand the struggles and successes of the black population. Essays such as "The Negro Artist and the Racial Mountain" (1926) and novels like *The Blacker the Berry* (1929) revealed a very human side of black Americans, intentionally aiming to improve world perceptions. Countee Cullen's impressive collection of poetry, fiction, and plays spoke boldly and candidly on the impact racist attitudes have had on the Black psyche.

Blues music influenced Langston Hughes writings about urban black life and Zora Neale Hurston's essays and short fictions reflected richness in racial heritage (see Appendix). Authors like Jessie Redmon Fauset and Nella Larsen explored racial identity and middle-class life in their short stories. Magazines and newspapers owned by black Americans allowed for free expression and freed the writers from the constricting influences of white society. Publicity in these publications broadened the reach and impact of the movement.

So, while racial discrimination in the 1920s still kept business and professional career doors closed to blacks, in the arts, they were thriving as never before. This was especially true in show business.

Music and Performers

Music created during the Harlem Renaissance gave the public another way to explore the world of black Americans. Inspired by the themes, melodies, and rhythms of the Southern spirituals, composers blessed the world with catchy renditions of blues and jazz, now being spread far beyond Harlem through film, studio recordings, and radio. For New Yorkers, the Cotton Club, the Apollo Theater, and the Savoy became increasingly popular with both black and white audiences. Performers like Duke Ellington, Billie Holliday, Bessie Smith (see Appendix A), and Cab Calloway gave these new genres of music a permanent place in the American songbook.

Josephine Baker (Figure 3.1), Bill "Bojangles" Robinson, Jelly Roll Morton, Paul Robeson, and Louis Armstrong drew sell-out crowds, both in and outside of Harlem. While jazz and blues may have been the most popular music to be born of the Harlem Renaissance (Shaw 1989), classical musicians like Marian Anderson and Harry Burleigh were also able to break down racial barriers at symphonic concerts. And singers Paul Robeson (see Appendix A) and Adelaide Hall did the same at Broadway theaters.

The Renaissance also produced the Lindy Hop—a swing dance influenced by the Charleston, jazz, and tap—and versions of the Viennese Waltz (see Appendix A). Both the dances and music became wildly popular outside the black communities, and even began to win fans in Europe. Exposure in both black and mainstream media drove that success. As they grew in fame and respectability in the entertainment world, winning favor with

Figure 3.1 Josephine Baker: Biography.com (www.biography.com/people/josephine-baker-9195959)

crowds and critics alike, the Harlem-based performers toured the world—spreading the story of the Harem Renaissance with every note they played.

Art

Many of the greatest works of the Harlem Renaissance were in the form of paintings and sculpture. Black American artists had rarely created art reflective of black American subject matter prior to their immigration north. But by the end of the 1920s, the artists developed unique, personal styles portraying black American culture and the traditions of Africa. Artists helped dispel the popular Negro stereotypes by portraying their subjects as sensitive, intelligent, and dignified. At the same time, they infused their works with images of Africa and themes of racial pride.

As with musicians and writers of the period, the Harlem painters, illustrators, and sculptors used their art as yet another platform to tell the story of black Americans. Their works, and the attention it received, demonstrated the enormous contribution black Americans were making to American culture.

Aaron Douglas, a prominent painter, created his own style by using black American men and women, often painted in silhouette form, reflecting imagery from the day's most popular novels and essays. Critics praised his works for their ability to evoke both a spiritual yearning and racial pride among his readers.

Artist Laura Wheeler Waring created portraits and still life images of well-known black American individuals during this time period. She also created illustrations in magazines promoting the intelligent, beautiful, and sophisticated black American.

Artists Richmond Barthe and Meta Warrick Fuller created sculptures with an African style but highlighting the beauty of black Americans. (The "Black is Beautiful" concept would emerge some 30 years later.) Paintings of black American life were portrayed in a variety of perspectives and styles.

Paris Migration

Many of the more successful artists eventually left Harlem for the world's cultural Mecca, Paris, claiming the move would allow them to flourish even more (Etherington-Smith 2015). Black American culture could be seen, heard, and felt throughout the City of Light. Much to the surprise of these new Parisians, the music, art, dance, poetry, and photography they had created once in uptown Manhattan were now on full display in Paris's most fashionable neighborhoods.

A New Black Middle Class

Though the Harlem Renaissance was primarily a creative movement, education and economic progress for black Americans was also essential. As a new middle class emerged in major cities, including Detroit, Chicago, Cleveland, and New York City, property and business ownership became critical in shaping the new black middle class. Black churches also bought property to help spur the development of Harlem, while groups financed home ownership and business development to improve the economic standing of the black American community.

Lasting Impact

The Harlem Renaissance, as influential and embedded as it had become in American culture, ended soon after the Stock Market crash of 1929. As the Great Depression hit, jobs disappeared and the dour mood of the country shifted, practically overnight, from entertainment to economic survival.

Although the Harlem Renaissance ended in the early 1930s, the movement has had an impact for decades, shaping the identity of black Americans, and helping them continue to gain acceptance in what is still, in many parts of America, a racially divided society.

The artists who came of age in the post-World War II era ushered in a new group to pick up were their forebears left off.

With the help of television, radio performers like Ray Charles, Sammy Davis Jr., Billie Holliday, Ella Fitzgerald, Sarah Vaughan, Lena Horne, and Dinah Washington became immediate hits with a worldwide audience. So accepted as an integral part of the post-war culture, they are now considered not as black American performers, but as American performers. With social media and streaming music services, they are more popular than ever. Just as dances like the Lindy Hop grew in popularity during the Harlem Renaissance, new dances emerged a decade later: the Jitterbug, Jive, Bop, and the Boogie-woogie. James Baldwin, Frederick Douglass, Richard Wright, Lorraine Hansberry, Ralph Ellison, and Gwendolyn Brooks continued to document their experiences and the social lives of black Americans in their books and articles. The Harlem Renaissance provided creative expression to the movements that followed: Civil Rights, Women's Equality, and Black Art, and has continued to influence artists, performers, and writers today.

Conclusion

The Harlem Renaissance movement promoted black American identity, pride, and self-awareness. While black Americans had virtually no voice during the early 20th century, the Harlem Renaissance gave them a voice that could be heard across all borders through melody, writing, and art. Not only did it enrich the nation's culture with new genres of original art, the movement created an identity for black Americans that had been inconceivable only a few years prior to the Northern Migration. The exposure gained from presentations, essays, newspaper, and magazine coverage, and eventually radio, television, and the Internet fueled the movement and made its enormous impact possible.

Takeaway

While literature, music, and art might not traditionally be thought of as public relations techniques, they point out the value of using both action and communication as a key to effecting positive social change. The works produced during the Harlem Renaissance challenged the common stereotypes much of the United States held about African Americans in the 1920s. The works of art likely did more to improve public attitudes about African Americans than any planned, professionally run public relations campaigns that came before or after.

The Harlem Renaissance provided a platform to tell the rest of the world about the social injustices and economic hardships African Americans faced. Through dance, film, jazz, and novels, the artists conveyed stories with hard-hitting emotional appeal. We know today that striking an emotional chord with an audience is a far more effective way to impact attitudes than reason and logic alone.

The Harlem Renaissance enabled dozens of artists to climb out of poverty. This created, for the first time in American history, a large group of successful role models for the rest of the African American community. The fame of these artists—whether seen on screen, heard over radio, or seen in news coverage—conveyed an important message to the rest of the African American community: that success was possible for them too. Equally important, perhaps, is the enormous role it played in influencing both perceptions and behavior within the white population.

In hindsight, the Northern Migration, and the Harlem Renaissance that emerged from it, may well have set the tone for the civil rights era decades later. Using the arts as a communications tool showed African Americans that influencing public opinion was, indeed, possible.

CHAPTER 4

Michael Sam Makes Great Gains for the LGBT Movement

Before February 2014, discussions of Lesbian, Gay, Black, and Transgender (LGBT) rights in America had largely focused on same-sex marriage. At the same time, though, LGBT Americans considered employment discrimination to be a top priority (Brown 2013). One ongoing area of employment concern was the exclusion, and support of, openly gay athletes in professional sports.

While public sentiment and policy toward LGBT individuals has changed greatly over the last decade, and entertainment celebrities have come out publicly more and more, professional sports has often been labeled "the closet" in America (Chibbaro 2013). While athletes themselves have been coming out more often in recent years, many of these athletes have announced their sexual identity after retiring from their professional careers (Edwards 2013).

The ability for LGBT athletes to be publicly "out" has been an important goal for the LGBT movement for a number of reasons. First, athletes are often high-profile figures, thus able to bring great attention to the movement. Second, the very notion that LGBT individuals can be professional athletes helps break down cultural stereotypes, especially those associated with gay men ("IU Expert on Sport and Masculinity Says Michael Sam Case Challenges 'Old School' Norms" 2014).

In February 2014, the movement faced an important moment when Michael Sam, the co-defensive player of the year in college football's most prolific conference—the Southeastern Conference (SEC)—came out publicly as gay (Connlley 2014). Sam's announcement predated his attempts to be drafted that spring into the National Football League (NFL). The issue became how could the LGBT movement support such a brave individual without interfering with his professional potential? At the same time, how could the movement use such an important moment to facilitate broader conversations about LGBT athletes, as well as LGBT individuals and stereotypes?

To find the answers to these questions, organizations turned to public relations as the profession best suited for the job, and that not only took advantage of new technologies but also reached a diversity of publics.

Background

Few areas of public opinion have changed as quickly and dramatically as American views toward LGBT individuals over the last few decades ("Gay and Lesbian Rights" n.d.). For years, media coverage and research about the LGBT movement focused almost exclusively on same-sex marriage, at the expense of many other issues. Following a Hawaii court ruling in 1993, which implied same-sex individuals may have legal paths to marriage rights, the U.S. Congress passed the Defense of Marriage Act, which ensured that states would not have to validate marriages granted in other states ("Baehr v. Miike" n.d.; Socarides 2013, March 13). The measure easily passed, as 85 Senators ("On Passage of the Bill" (h.r. 3396) 1996) and over three-fourths of the House of Representatives ("On Passage Defense of Marriage Act" (h.r. 3396) 1996) voted for it.

Beyond marriage, American views toward LBGT individuals have long been negative. As recently as the 1980s, the Supreme Court upheld a state's right to criminalize homosexual acts between consenting adults (Goldstein 1988). American public opinion at the time mirrored the Court's sentiment, as only about one-third of Americans thought homosexuality should be legal in 1986 ("Gay and Lesbian Rights" n.d.). It was not until 2003 that the Court ruled in *Lawrence v. Texas* that states could not arrest adults for having consensual same-sex relationships (Tribe 2004). Following the decision, though, still only about half of Americans agreed with the Court that same-sex *relations* should be legal at all ("Gay and Lesbian Rights" n.d.), let alone recognizing *marriage* rights for such individuals. Voter initiatives from the end of the 1990s until North Carolina in 2012 resulted in same-sex marriage bans via state constitutional amendments ("History and Timeline of the Freedom to Marry in the United States" 2015). And yet, the tide of American sentiment dramatically changed in just a few years. By 2015, the Supreme Court ensured that same-sex relationships were constitutionally protected, granting gay and lesbian Americans the right to marry in all 50 states (Obergefell v. Hodges 2015). Following the decision, over two-thirds of Americans now held the opinion that same-sex relations should be legal ("Gay and Lesbian Rights" n.d.).

Same-sex marriage received significant attention over the last two decades, and a number of culturally important moments related to celebrity, entertainment, and American sport increased the issue's visibility. In the late 1990s, Ellen DeGeneres caused a great uproar and the flight of advertisers when a character she played on her sitcom announced that she was a lesbian, complementing DeGeneres' own public coming out (Adhikari and Francis 2012). After the announcement, the show's ratings quickly fell, and it was canceled the next season in mid-1998 (Carter 1998). That fall, NBC aired what became a hit show, *Will & Grace*, a program with two prominent gay characters (Battles and Hilton-Morrow 2002). By 2003, even amidst one of the peaks of anti-LGBT public sentiment seen in marriage ballot initiatives, DeGeneres was back, hosting her own daytime talk show ("This Day in History" n.d.). The show was a huge success for DeGeneres, on the air for over a decade with no sign of stopping (Andreeva 2013). It served as another measure of progress for the movement.

The movement has long fought to change perceptions and opinions about LGBT individuals by protecting and supporting them in the workplace. In the 1970s, Harvey Milk, the first openly gay person to be elected to public office in California, famously helped lead an initiative to combat efforts that were attempting to remove LBGT individuals from working in public schools (Griffin and Ouellett 2003). The initiative sparked an opportunity for gays and lesbians to come out to their friends, families, and coworkers in an attempt to change people's perceptions of LGBT individuals ("The Official Harvey Milk Biography" n.d.). Decades later, (Crandall 2012) the movement fought attempts to ban gays and lesbians from the military, resulting in the often criticized "Don't Ask, Don't Tell" policy, put into effect in 1993. Critics argued the military environment was no place for "social experimentation." But, as another sign of progress, less than two decades later, the policy was fully repealed in 2011 under the tenure of the Obama administration (Bumiller 2011). The change marked another important moment for the movement, not only in terms of policy, but also in terms of breaking down stigmas and stereotypes. Gays and lesbians could now publicly demonstrate that they could be, and were, American military heroes, just as their heterosexual peers.

In recent years, attention within the movement has also turned toward supporting LGBT athletes in sports and professional athletic workplace environments. Groups such as the LGBT Sports Coalition were formed to end discrimination against LGBT persons in sports ("About" n.d.). Organizations such as Athlete Ally ("Our Story" n.d.) and the You Can Play Project ("Out Cause" n.d.) were also created to promote inclusiveness, equality, and support of LBGT athletes. And, LGBT-focused media outlets working with the LGBT Sports Coalition, such as *Outsports*, have made it their mission to promote LGBT athletes' coming out stories at every level in an attempt to "open sports for everyone," thus allowing "the institution of sports. . .[to be] a model for inclusion. . ." (Zeigler 2015).

The movement's focus on LGBT individuals in sports has arguably had many of the same goals and benefits as the previous efforts to support LGBT teachers in the workplace or gays in the military. By showing that LGBT athletes not only exist, but can also excel in sports, the movement has sought to change broader public sentiment about LGBT people. For example, these athletes often counter stereotypes that gay men are "less masculine" than heterosexual males (Goodman 2014). Similarly, gay African American athletes, such as Jason Collins, have created opportunities to discuss the intersection of sexuality and race ("The Role of Race in Jason Collins' Coming-Out Story" n.d.). These efforts have also focused on the positive impact such athletes can have on LGBT youth (Waldron 2014). It was not until 2013 that Major League Soccer (MLS), among America's highest profile male sports leagues, had an active openly gay player in Robbie Rogers (Witz 2013). The same year, the National Basketball Association's (NBA) Jason Collins became that league's first player to come out while still active (ESPN.com News Services 2013).

Yet, following the announcement, Collins, a seasoned veteran, remained unsigned until February 2014 (Youngmisuk, Shelburne, and Stein 2014).

The Announcement

While these moments obtained great attention, Collins was at the end of his career, and Rogers was playing in a league that obtains far less attention than the *Big Four*: football, basketball, baseball, and hockey. The question became when would the nation's most popular league—the NFL—have its first openly gay player? (Levy 2013)

Such an event was considered paramount to the LGBT sports movement, as an openly gay athlete in the nation's most popular—and perhaps most brutal—sport could help epitomize the movement's goals of breaking down stereotypes while offering another high-profile role model for LGBT youth. Movement organizations thus had an opportunity and challenge when, in February 2014, Michael Sam, an award-winning college athlete, publicly announced that he was a gay man.

While Michael Sam had come out to his team before his senior season at the University of Missouri, there were few indications that the information had spread much beyond the team or local city. But, by the Senior Bowl in January 2014—where athletes attempt to impress scouts before the NFL Draft held in May—it became clear that some scouts were aware of Sam's sexuality. Sam's management team wanted to get ahead of the story. As Zeigler (2014, February 9) points out, the team included public relations counselor Howard Bragman, an expert in handling public coming out stories. They orchestrated a campaign to have the athlete sit down with handpicked outlets to break the news. Respected journalist John Branch had an interview with Sam in the *New York Times*. ESPN's Chris Connelly sat down with Sam for a broadcast story. And LGBT outlet *Outsports* covered the behind-the-scenes story of why Sam came out when, as well as the way, he did.

Initial coverage focused on the importance of the moment, as well as personal details, such as Sam's difficult upbringing (Connelly 2014; Branch 2014). His childhood included siblings who had been killed, died at a young age, gone missing or were in prison, and difficulties between Sam and his parents (Drape, Eder, and Witz 2014). Sam emphasized, "I want to own my truth," his management team noting that he wanted to be known as "a football player, not an activist" (Zeigler 2014, February 9). Accordingly, Sam's publicist informed LGBT-advocacy groups that they would not have access to the athlete; instead, Sam's "role in the movement" would be to be a football player who happened to be a proud gay man, not an activist who happened to be a football player.

Zeigler (2014, February 9) continues by noting that as movement organizations agreed not to get Sam involved as an activist, their role in the story might have appeared to be limited. And yet, these organizations were able to use the culturally important moment to facilitate broader discussions about LGBT athletes in sports, advance relationships with professional leagues and players, and develop messaging that combatted stereotypes and inspired LGBT youth.

Strategic Insights

Even though the movement had come quite far by 2014, the fact that the nation's most popular sport still did not have an openly out player spoke to ongoing societal attitudes toward LGBT people. The persistence of stereotypes and examples of homophobia were easily seen. For example, the antigay Westboro Baptist Church protested at the University of Missouri campus during an event that was being held to honor the football team's previous season (Mandell 2014). Meanwhile, a Washington, DC, lobbyist floated the idea of drafting a congressional bill that would ban gay athletes from the NFL (Shabad 2014). While these more extreme examples obtained plenty of attention, initial audience feedback seen on news pages and on social media also demonstrated how much homophobia still remained in society. Negative, vulgar, and even racist comments were directed not only at Sam, but also gay individuals more broadly (Cabosky 2015). Feedback also portrayed stereotypes that needed to be challenged, such as notions that masculinity is exclusively linked to heterosexuality or that gay men or gay role models are all white and affluent (Smith 2014).

From a media perspective, beyond covering the historic nature of the moment, early coverage often focused on topics such as how Sam would fit in the locker room, (Connelly 2014; Schalter 2014), coupled with attempts to report on any negative comments coaches or other players would say about a gay athlete (Cabosky 2015; Hanzus 2014).

For example, just days before Sam's public announcement, New Orleans Saints player Jason Vilma had obtained plenty of attention for saying he would not feel comfortable showering next to a gay player (Sieczkowski 2014). Upon Sam's announcement, the story instantly reappeared (Branch2014). Coverage from *Sports Illustrated* that entirely relied on anonymous sources from team officials and staff also drove much of the narrative after sources said they thought the league might not be ready for a gay player, some even saying Sam would not be drafted at all (King 2014). Popular gossip sites like *TMZ* also attempted to promote salaciousness by distributing images of Sam dancing at a gay bar, even though the images were from months before Sam's announcement (TMZ Staff 2014). Thus, movement organizations would have to combat these narratives.

Organizations such as Athlete Ally and the You Can Play Project engaged in strategies that go far beyond media relations, developing close relationships with "third party groups," including professional leagues, teams, and players (McQuade 2012). The organizations helped develop, educate, and train officials and players from these organizations. To do that, movement organizations needed to be knowledgeable about their stakeholders. They had to understand football, teams, and locker room culture to effectively build an open and supportive environment, not only for Michael Sam, but for any future gay athlete (Cabosky 2015).

During high-profile moments for the LGBT movement, advocacy organizations also often focus on the impact on LGBT youth (Adam 2014). For example, movement organizations have worked with celebrities and athletes to promote the GLAAD (formerly the Gay & Lesbian Alliance Against Defamation) Spirit Day, an annual event that focuses on bringing an end to bullying (Fabian 2013). Similarly, when high-profile sports figures have drawn media scrutiny for making homophobic remarks, movement organizations have responded with discussions about creating a safe environment for families and youth ("GLAAD Calls on MLB, Atlanta Braves to Take Action After Atlanta Braves Coach Roger McDowell Uses Anti-Gay Slurs, Makes Violent Threats at Game" 2011). With so much media attention on Michael Sam, organizations had a substantial opportunity to reach out to LGBT youth.

Public Relations Programs

With these realities and insights, movement organizations responded to Michael Sam's announcement with messaging and public relations tactics designed to bring about attitudinal and cultural change.

As soon as Sam's announcement was made, news outlets of all types discussed the topic, as well as the situation for LGBT athletes in sport more broadly. Groups like GLAAD and the You Can Play Project's Wade Davis were prepared and made themselves readily available (Bolles 2014, February 12).

The day before the Sunday announcement, Sam's management and public relations team had pulled together a few key individuals to meet with the athlete privately at Howard Bragman's house. The group included many former professional athletes who were now openly gay, such as Wade Davis, as well straight athletes who were LGBT allies. Zeigler, the cofounder of *Outsports*, was also present to help Sam practice for interviews. The group was not only able to offer their support to Sam before the news broke, but they also had the opportunity to meet the athlete themselves before discussing him with the American public.

Over the years, GLAAD has developed strong ties to media outlets, making them a go-to source during moments like Sam's announcement. GLAAD's President, Sarah Kate Ellis, was featured in interviews with "over 40 media outlets," including influential and wide-reaching sources, such as The Huffington Post, *USA Today*, and MSNBC. In many of these interviews, the organization partnered with Wade Davis (Bolles 2014, February 11). As a former NFL professional himself, Davis was able to offer strong insights into what the moment meant for the league, players, and other gay athletes (Bolles 2014, February 12). GLAAD emphasized how a moment such as this was an opportunity for the movement:

> The media buzz around Michael Sam's coming out presented a substantial opportunity to talk about LGBT people in sports and culture. His coming out received significant media attention, giving GLAAD and partners like You Can Play the opportunity to send a strong message about LGBT inclusion in sports. (Bolles 2014, February 12)

Within these media relations opportunities, GLAAD and Davis promoted strategic *message frames*. Bolles analyzed one frame that advanced the notion that professional football was "ready for an openly gay player" (2014, February 12). In response to debates about locker room comfort, Sarah Kate Ellis said, "There has been a lot of talk about the locker room, and I think that's a reliance on an outdated stereotype." She continued by comparing the situation to debates about the military, "I remember hearing that argument when 'Don't Ask, Don't Tell' was being debated, and we can see now firsthand that gay service members who can serve openly are only helping the military and it hasn't been an issue." These arguments thus combatted notions that working with gay athletes would cause a distraction, situating the claims by comparing the moment to historical cases.

GLAAD and Davis also employed messages about how Sam's story had the opportunity to demonstrate to LGBT youth "that they can grow up to be anything they want to be, including an NFL player" (Bolles 2014, February 12). Davis additionally told how Sam's race could send a particular message to some LGBT youth:

> Michael is first and foremost a talented football player. . . . His story sends a message to LGBT young people, especially young black men, that you are free to show up in the world as your authentic self and others will embrace you. (Adam 2014).

Beyond having a strong voice in traditional media outlets, movement organizations were also able to spread their message to broader stakeholders through their strategic use of social media platforms. Efforts with traditional mainstream outlets, such as the *New York Time*s and popular broadcast news programs were complemented with the use of social media channels (GLAAD, Twitter Page). The Human Rights Campaign, whose political policy focus would seemingly have little to do with Michael Sam, was able to drive support for the athlete through its two million followers on Facebook alone, a number that dwarfs most modern television news programs (Human Rights Campaign, Facebook Page).

Individual organizations were able to drive their own narratives on their own channels, advancing words of encouragement for Sam (Athlete Ally 2014). These efforts also demonstrated the hybridity—or the cross between separate groups (Wikipedia n.d.)—of modern media as organizations used social media channels to further distribute content that originally occurred in other media, allowing them to spread messages with pro-LGBT frames that were created by other sources (GLAAD, Twitter 2014, February 12).

One of the most prominent examples of this media hybridity was seen in the promotion of a video commentary made by a local sportscaster, Dale Hansen. A veteran Dallas journalist from conservative Texas, Hansen was not the type of person expected to offer a commentary that would define Michael Sam's coming out announcement. Hansen admitted in an on-air commentary that he was "not always comfortable when a man tells me he's gay." He continued, "I don't understand his world." And yet, Hansen gave an impassioned commentary decrying the reports that some in the league thought Sam's draft stock would drop because they thought gay athletes might not fit well in a locker room. Hansen claimed hypocrisy, noting that the league was filled with players who were convicted of violent crimes or drug use. Comparing the culturally defining moment to times when African American athletes were not able to play in professional leagues, Hansen said it was time for attitudes to change, claiming that "it's time to celebrate [Sam] now." The speech became a defining commentary that shaped Sam's announcement (Cabosky 2015). Hansen's commentary initially aired on a local TV station, but a YouTube copy of the video was quickly picked up by queer news outlets (Zeigler 2014, February 12) and distributed through social media channels by movement organizations, such as GLAAD (2014, February 12) and the HRC ("Human Rights Campaign" 2014). The video was viewed by over 4.9 million viewers on YouTube alone (Cabosky 2015).

It gained further attention when it was re-tweeted by DeGeneres (2014), an LGBT celebrity with over 45 million followers on Twitter. DeGeneres then invited Hansen onto her daytime talk show, reaching millions more (Nichols 2014). And so, a commentary that called for society and the NFL to change was able to drive a forceful narrative as movement organizations and leading LGBT figures were able to use multiple forms of media to spread pro-LGBT frames (Cabosky 2015).

The dissemination of pro-LGBT commentaries, such as Hansen's, also demonstrated how movement organizations were strategically able to use third-party influencers and allies to broaden the voice of the movement.

Organizations used social media to further the reach of statements in support of Sam made by influential figures such as President Barack Obama (GLAAD 2014, February 10), as well as other athletes, such as famous NFL player Donte Stallworth (Athletic Ally 2014, February 10) and tennis player Andy Roddick (Athletic Ally 2014, February 19). Athlete Ally used its connections with straight athletes to further the equality message. In some instances, straight allied athletes wrote blog pieces (Ayanbadejo 2014) while others wrote guest columns in mainstream outlets (Barwin 2014). Others were used as sources in influential news pieces in venues such as *Time* (Gregory 2014), their voices able to advance messages of equality and to promote the idea that the league was ready for the inclusion of openly gay athletes. These third-party influencers not only allowed pro-LGBT frames to spread, but they also arguably offered an important sense of authenticity, especially as allied NFL athletes could speak to how locker rooms were ready for gay players (Barwin 2014).

NFL Internal Communications

Michael Sam's announcement became an important catalyst to promote further educational and relationship-building programs within the NFL, as well as other professional leagues.

You Can Play Project's Wade Davis' status as a former NFL athlete gave him an important insider perspective, allowing him the ability to more effectively bring about changes in attitudes and perceptions among league officials and players (Davis 2015). While some in the LGBT community often criticized and attacked league individuals who made homophobic comments, Davis said this was the wrong approach. He argued that, if a player makes an anti-LGBT comment, it is instead an "opportunity" to change views. According to Davis, if a player gets criticized by those on the outside, "the rest of the guys in the locker room will close in ranks, because it is a family, it is a community, and they will protect each other more often than right or wrong."

Thus, when a player or official makes a homophobic remark, Davis often gets called in. Using his strong knowledge of his target public, his goal is not to attack the individual, but instead to speak with them one-on-one in an attempt to change their attitudes by sharing a new perspective with them. And yet, all of this access for the movement came about because Davis had spent years building up trust between himself, the league, and the LGBT community.

Following Sam's announcement, the NFL brought in Davis to speak at a meeting with team owners and coaches to share with them how they could create a positive work environment for gay athletes (Associated Press 2014). Teams like the St. Louis Rams—the team that drafted Michael Sam—also brought in Davis to speak with their players and coaches (Wagoner 2014). Davis' message advanced the notion that LGBT athletes should be treated no different than other players. The approach's effectiveness in bringing about change was evident. During his meeting with the Rams, Davis said the first question Sam's teammates asked was, "How do we support Michael?" And, at the presentation with league owners and coaches, Davis earned positive feedback (Jones 2014). Denver Broncos coach John Fox told ESPN that Davis' presentation prioritized the issue for him, calling it "eye-opening" (Legwold 2014). Fox summarized that "it was the most incredible presentation" he'd seen since he had been in the league.

To bring about effective change during times such as Sam's coming out, Davis (2015) said, "I don't believe the media is the best place to go." Instead, Davis' use of relationship building, trust, and small group and one-on-one communication proved to be quite effective at bringing about new understandings of LGBT athletes in the locker room (Davis, 2015).

Conclusion

Sam's story clearly gave adults, fellow athletes, and young people hope. Much like Harvey Milk's calls for LGBT individuals to come out to their families, friends, and coworkers, Sam's public admission became a catalyst for countless others to follow his lead and come out.

One such story that received wide attention was shared on the University of Missouri Facebook page, a post from a father who told of his son's coming out in front of the family after Michael Sam had been drafted by the St. Louis Rams (Zeigler 2014, May 12). The post, which was further shared by news sources, read,

> I sat in front of my television and watched the NFL draft with my father (a Master Sergeant in the U.S. Army), my brother (U.S. Army Special Forces), my son (whose parents are both soldiers) in a room of hardened veterans with over 85 years of military service and more than 15 combat tours. I saw true courage. When Michael Sam was finally drafted, my 15-year-old son started crying and told me he was gay. He said he didn't want to hide anymore or be embarrassed about who he was. Thank you Mizzou for embracing Mr. Sam and recruiting a young man of his caliber so that kids like my son have more positive role models to look to . . . and thank you for providing opportunities to students regardless of diversity . . . your program is truly a class act from the players to the coaching staff! I'll be pulling for you. Stay Classy, Mizzou!

The effects of Sam's moment rippled through athletic programs across the nation. By August, *The Washington Blade* had reported that Sam's announcement had "inspire[d] college athletes to come out," noting that other college football and basketball players, swimmers and the like had mustered the courage to be open and honest with themselves and those around them (Lavers 2014). And so, with each story, with each coming out, the world was changing, one locker room at a time.

The Michael Sam story serves as an example of how public relations is not limited to media relations between an organization and news outlets. In fact, Sam's tale served as an example of how public relations goes far beyond the relationship between organizations and publics. Public relations scholar Maureen Taylor writes of public relations' ability to create social capital, or the value of "relationships and networks of information sharing" (Taylor 2011, February 10).

In the Sam story, while organizations were sometimes at the center of these relationships, there were many other important actors that brought about new attitudes and the dissemination of information. Many individuals—such as Ellen DeGeneres, local commentators like Dale Hansen, or even the collection of everyday Americans who shared their stories online or to their families and friends—played a part in developing this social capital.

Takeaway

This campaign employed many of the same tools as historical grassroots social movements: role models, relationship building, third party influencers, and tie-ins with established organizations. But unlike social movements of the past, the campaign in support of Michael Sam benefited from contemporary advances in public relations.

First and foremost, it benefited tremendously by using Twitter and other forms of social media to disseminate and share repeated messages within the LGBT community—a very vocal and influential audience, and one with its own only media outlets.

Second, the campaign employed carefully crafted "message frames"—a sophisticated communications approach that conveys to an audience not just *what* to think about but *how* to think about it. One such frame used in the campaign—"professional football is ready for an openly gay player"—was highly persuasive to a mass audience.

Finally, it happened in an era increasingly sympathetic to LGBT causes. By 2014, the majority of the United States had already shown widespread acceptance to LGBT issues. It was just a matter of time before the last bastion of acceptance, the "macho" world of football, would be accepting as well.

After extensive strategic planning, the communications team, with the help of outside counsel, mounted a carefully orchestrated, multielement campaign, that concurrently impacted a wide variety of audiences, both internal and external.

Michael Sam's story epitomizes how a strategically crafted messaging campaign can not only change attitudes, it can help do away with society's stereotypes and prejudices, and create an environment more accepting of all people.

CHAPTER 5

The War on Tobacco

What chance does a grassroots antismoking campaign really have against the sophisticated, sleek communications, and moneyed coffers of big tobacco companies? Smoking is seductive, ritualistic, and social. Characters chain smoke contemplatively in 1960s' French New Wave cinema. Rough and tumble iconic smokers graced American television and film for years. Cigarettes practically sell themselves. As BR, the fictional tobacco salesman shouts in the movie *Thank You for Smoking*, "We don't sell Tic Tacs, we sell cigarettes. And they're cool, available, and addictive! The job is almost done for us!" (*Thank You for Smoking* quotes 2015).

Beyond the smoke and mirrors of big tobacco's glamor stands a grim reality: each year, smoking kills six million people worldwide; smoking is also the cause of respiratory illnesses for thousands of others ("Fast Facts About Smoking" 2015). In the United States, it is the largest preventable killer and is responsible for more deaths than from car accidents, illegal drugs, murder, and AIDS combined ("Toll of Tobacco in the U.S. Fact Sheet" 2015). In addition to death, tobacco use leads to premature aging, rotting teeth, hair loss, sagging skin, and yellow eyes ("Fast Fact About Smoking" 2015). And smoking causes a substantial burden to national health care costs. Tobacco costs the United States more than $170 billion in health care expenditures and $151 billion in lost productivity each year (Xu *et al.* 2014).

While public relations and advertising contributed to the rise of the tobacco business (Public Relations Museum. Videos of Edward Bernays n.d.), the same tactics used to help promote tobacco have worked well to reverse the growth of smoking. Coupled with leadership from the medical community, antitobacco advocates have used public relations strategies and tactics to help change public attitudes toward smoking, raise awareness about the health risks, and promote the policy regulations required for lasting change ("Achievements in Public Health, 1900–1999: Tobacco Use—United States, 1900–1999" 1999).

In its efforts to shape policy and reduce smoking worldwide, the antitobacco movement has had to compete with the ever creative and resource-rich tobacco industry. One successful approach has been to use former smokers to speak out against the tobacco industry. Today anti-smoking advocates use sleek ads aimed at teen and young adults, with a goal of leveraging the socially minded Millennial generation to try to stop the next generation from smoking.

Public relations campaigns exposing the risks of smoking have led to stronger legislative action restricting tobacco sales, protection against consumers from deceptive marketing practices, and public awareness campaigns that have contributed to the decline of smoking in the United States. But the tobacco industry still finds ways to expand to countries where smoking is tied directly into the national economy. Understanding the strategies of those efforts can help shape future activities to combat the resurgence of smoking.

This chapter analyzes the fight to change public perception, starting with the Surgeon General's landmark study issued in 1964, that declared smoking a public health risk, to the present ("50th Anniversary: Surgeon General's Report on Smoking" 2015). It examines tactics led by anti-smoking groups, particularly the American Legacy Foundation, which runs the innovative youth tobacco prevention campaign *truth* (Bradley and Nichols 2014). Also explored is the evolution of the antitobacco movement's messages over the past decades, in order to analyze which of those strategies can be used to advance current antismoking efforts, particularly in light of the rise in electronic cigarettes.

Smoking—A Known Health Risk

In 1964, the U.S. Surgeon General published a landmark study that linked smoking to cancer. The report officially declared smoking a public health issue, and led to a wave of civic action against the industry. While it was the first time that the U.S. government and the medical community established a firm position against smoking, the threat caused by cigarettes had been discussed well before then.

The first attempts to curb tobacco use can be traced back to the early 1600s. In 1604, King James I of England published an antitobacco tract, "A Counterblast to Tobacco" (which modern public relations professionals would call a "white paper"). It illustrated his disdain for the product and particularly for tobacco smoking. Surprisingly, he also made reference to what we now know to be secondhand smoking; however, his critiques of tobacco use were primarily based on moral and hygienic reasoning rather than health concerns. Unfortunately, mass media and social media did not exist in his day, and as a result, his effort did not slow down the consumption of tobacco, which continued to grow in its various uses for cigar smoking, pipe smoking, chewing, and inhaling as snuff ("Reducing Tobacco Use, A Report of the Surgeon General" Chapter 2).

The introduction of mass-produced cigarettes in the 1840s fueled their popularity and as a result, drew a more critical response from the public. The growth in sales coincided with a growing movement throughout America for health reform, and antitobacco sentiment was a common topic in writings at the time.

At the same time, the desire for health consciousness was woven together with religion. The Seventh-Day Adventists used public relations techniques to champion tobacco abstention in the late 1840s and early 1850s, culminating in the publications of articles attacking "the filthy, health-destroying, God-dishonoring practice of using tobacco" (Numbers 2008, p. 86). A large number of individuals and newly formed groups also began to speak out against the rise in tobacco addiction. The American Anti-Tobacco Society was founded in 1849, which today we would call an "advocacy group." George Trask, founder of the Society, was known as the "Anti-Tobacco Apostle." He encouraged young people to take his "Band of Hope" pledge: "I hereby solemnly promise to abstain from the use of all Intoxicating Liquors as a beverage; I also promise to abstain from the use of Tobacco in all forms, and all Profane Language" (Jacob Sullum, "For Your Own Good: The Anti-Smoking Crusade," New York, 1998, p. 26).

Meanwhile in England, surgeon Samuel Solly sparked the Great Tobacco Controversy with his article "Clinical Lectures on Paralysis," published in 1856 in the Lancet medical magazine (Hilton 2000). His piece triggered a heated debate by linking the recent increase in tobacco consumption with cases of general paralysis that appeared to be cited more frequently. This article captured the attention of medical professionals and also helped catapult the topic into the mainstream.

In the United States, efforts toward the end of the 19th century focused on convincing youth—boys and young men—not to take up smoking. For example, the Consolidated Anti-Cigarette League was set up in New York City by the president of the Board of Education. Although he was a smoker himself, he tried to convince 25,000 schoolboys to pledge not to smoke until they turned 21 (Troyer and Markle 1983).

In 1912, Dr. Isaac Adler, an American doctor, was the first to make a strong connection between lung cancer and smoking in his research paper, "Primary Malignant Growth of the Lung and Bronchi," (Isaac Adler. "Primary Malignant Growth of the Lung and Bronchi". (1912) New York, Longmans, Green. pp. 3–12). Following this, in 1930, researchers in Dresden, Germany, made perhaps the strongest ever case against tobacco use, publishing the first-ever statistical correlation between cancer and smoking.

The publication of these medical advancements gave credence to the anti-smoking message of campaigners. The conversation now began to shift toward the substantial health risks that had now been proven as well as to various social arguments that had previously been overlooked or ignored. Nonetheless, starting at the turn of the century, smoking rates in the U.S. skyrocketed thanks to continued improvements in mass production and an explosion of mass media cigarette advertising ("Achievements in Public Health, 1900–1999" 1999). Annual per capita consumption grew from 54 in 1900 to 4,345 cigarettes in 1963 (a half pack a day per person). The growth continued until 1964—the year that the Surgeon General's landmark study linking smoking to health risks was published ("Surveillance for Selected Tobacco-Use Behaviors—United States, 1900–1994" 1994).

Cigarette smoking among women increased in the 1920s with the help of a public relations campaign conducted by one of the early leaders in public relations, Edward Bernays. He linked smoking to the women's movement, positioning cigarettes as "torches of freedom" and upending the social taboo against women smoking in public (Amos and Haglund 2000).

In 1929, Bernays orchestrated the widely publicized Easter Day marches in various cities across the country, featuring famous debutantes of the day boldly smoking cigarettes. He also shaped advertising messages that played into women's concerns about their weight. While his work advanced the goals of the women's movement, his work was primarily fueled by business interests. Removing the taboo against women smoking in public helped open a large market for his client, Lucky Strike (Amos and Haglund 2000). Bernays later tried to undo the damage his work had caused by advising public relations firms to stop working on behalf of the tobacco industry (Bisbort 2008).

Scientific studies linking tobacco use with cancer and associated health risks were published in the United States as early as the 1940s ("Achievements in Public Health, 1900–1999" 1999). However, advertising at the time suggested that the tobacco industry was aware of the connection to health risks as early as the 1920s. Ads featuring doctors alongside patients suggested that the medical community supported smoking. For example, a Lucky Strike ad from the 1920s positioned cigarettes as a slimming device. Yet the 1920 advertisement included disclaimer language. One ad with a shadowy image of an obese woman next to a thin woman says, "We do not say smoking *Lucky's* reduces flesh. We do say, when tempted to over-indulge, reach for a *Lucky* instead."

Lucky Strike also worked to differentiate itself from its competition by promoting its "toasted" method of curing tobacco, a method, it claimed, that can protect throats against irritation.

By the 1950s, Lucky Strike's ads had begun to feature dentists and athletes in addition to physicians. Despite the industry's use of such "role models" to endorse the use of cigarettes, the U.S. medical community was already starting to establish links between smoking and cancer. By 1919, lung cancer was such a rarely diagnosed disease that, at the Washington University's Barnes Hospital, an entire medical school class was invited to witness the autopsy of a man who had died from the disease. The professor leading the autopsy believed that no one in the class would ever again see another such case (Blum 1896–1981).

Dr. Alton Ochsner was among those students witnessing the lung autopsies. Nearly two decades later, he began to see an uptick of the once rare cancer. The patients all had a common thread: they had taken up smoking during World War I, when the now mass-advertised cigarettes were given out free to soldiers. In the trenches, soldiers didn't have time to savor a slow-burning cigar, or pack a pipe, so cigarettes became the go-to source for nicotine. They were even packed in the soldiers' food rations (Warner and Pollack 2014, November 13).

The 1950s—The "War on Tobacco" Begins

In the 1940s, Oschner began to publicize his theory that smoking was responsible for the increase in lung cancer. In 1952, he published an article in the *Journal of the American Medical Association* (JAMA) connecting science with his theory (Blum 1999). More and more such studies began to be published in the United States and in Britain. The JAMA published one of the most robust studies ever linking smoking to lung cancer; in 1952, *Readers Digest* published the JAMA findings in an article title "Cancer by the Carton" finally bringing the issue to the attention of the general public (Warner and Pollack 2014, November 13). However, by then, millions of Americans were smoking.

Soon the courts got involved. In 1954 Eva Cooper filed the first civil lawsuit against the tobacco industry. She sued R.J. Reynolds Tobacco Co. for the death of her husband from lung cancer. Cooper lost the case, but she became the first of a long line of litigants to put the industry on trial. Big Tobacco was forced to reveal what had long been hidden about its business practices and products (Curriden 1994). As these court battles ensued, the industry began facing mounting criticism from all sectors of the public.

To help counter the negative claims, tobacco companies started marketing improved filter and new low-tar formulations, promising a "healthier" smoke. Robert Proctor's 2012 book *Golden Holocaust* (Markel 2012), drawn on industry documents made public in litigation, shows how these cigarettes were never proven less dangerous, and were merely tactics created to assuage the public's fear.

The "War on Tobacco" began to gain traction in the late 1950s and led to a decade of strong, forceful action in the battle over public opinion and health. The tobacco industry fought back. In 1953, competitive cigarette companies came together to form the *Council for Tobacco Research* (later known as the *Tobacco Industry Research Committee* or TIRC).

TIRC began when Paul Hahn, president of the American Tobacco Company sent a telegram to eight other leading cigarette companies suggesting that they all work together as a single group to counter any government action against smoking ("A Brief History of the Council for Tobacco Research" 1982). This would give the industry a more unified voice, and one that, given its title, would appear to be less commercial.

The group was run by and out of the headquarters of the public relations firm Hill & Knowlton (H+K) in New York City.

Through the TIRC the cigarette industry was able to respond to negative publicity and fund prosmoking research. Though bound together publicly, many brands disagreed with the group's tactics. For example, Kent cigarettes chose to play into the public's health concerns by positioning its cigarettes as the "healthier choice." Other companies chose to vociferously deny any health risks and stay out of the debate altogether (Kluger 1997).

Lawyers counseling the industry advised that public acknowledgement of any culpability could open it up to regulation. But the industry felt it had to do something to show that it was aware of the public's concern. The TIRC rolled out rebuttal after rebuttal of cigarettes' links to disease. It produced articles for the general press to raise doubt about the medical findings with titles like "Heavy Smoker s with Low Mortality" (Timmins, William M. 1989, *Smoking and the Workplace: Issues and Answers for Human Resources Professionals*. New York: Praeger). It also used companies' annual reports and speeches to question tobacco's health hazards.

At the same time, in the face of mounting public health concerns, the industry's public relations firm advised its client to act responsibly. The firm proposed a campaign to voluntarily advise smokers to use the product in moderation and put health warnings on cigarette packages. They argued that such warnings would protect the companies from civil claims. But Lawyers feared it would be an admission (Kluger 1997). While the proposal did not gain any traction with the cigarette companies, warning labels were eventually mandated by government, a requirement that health organizations advocated for and secured.

Lawyers and public relations consultants reviewed every piece of public material in an effort to protect cigarette companies from litigation. But, no matter how much the industry spent on such counsel, it faced a relentless barrage of lawsuits, continuing to reveal its marketing and business practices.

The 1960s—The Decade that Put Tobacco on the Defense

While publicly denying the health risks (e.g., claiming there was no "evidence" that smoking posed health risks) and funding studies by "objective," credible medical institutions (e.g., the group gave a $25,000 three-year gift to Memorial Sloan-Kettering Cancer Center), Philip Morris was busy trying to engineer a "healthier" cigarette. In a laboratory memorandum dated November 15, 1961, Philip Morris researchers had confirmed trace amounts of 42 compounds in cigarette smoke identified as carcinogens. One of the researchers, Helmut Wakeham, produced a report titled "Research and Development Program Leading to a Medically Acceptable Cigarette" (Kluger 1997).

At the same time, the antismoking crusaders at the American Cancer Society joined forces with three other health groups—the National Heart Association, the National Tuberculosis Association, and the American Public Health Association—to pressure the newly elected president, John F. Kennedy, to address the growing public health concern. According to Kluger (1997), when their letters elicited no response from the White House, they threatened to go to the newspapers to complain about Kennedy's "foot-dragging." In 1961, reeling from the Bay of Pigs incident, President Kennedy could not afford any bad press. Kennedy referred the letters to his Health, Education and Welfare Secretary, who coordinated a meeting with the three organizations and the Surgeon General, Luther Terry. In 1962, President Kennedy was asked at a press conference what he was doing about the growing concern over smoking and health. He responded that he, himself, could not provide a satisfactory answer but that he would task the Surgeon General to work on the problem. Two weeks later, Surgeon General Terry announced there would be a committee formed to review the links between smoking and cancer.

Within two years, in 1964, the Surgeon General's committee released its findings on national television. Terry announced that the year-long study the committee had undertaken had indeed revealed a link to lung cancer. He declared that smoking was a public health issue, one of the most dangerous risks facing the country. The following day the Surgeon General's report was the lead story on radio, TV, and newspapers throughout the country.

The report remained one of the top news stories of 1964. The antitobacco advocacy groups finally had a strategic win in their war on smoking. But they picked a battle against a strong adversary. In 1964, the tobacco industry was an $8 billion a year industry responsible for $3 billion in local, state, and federal taxes, as well as 96,000 jobs and $150 million in advertising ("Blowing Smoke: The Lost Legacy of the Surgeon General's Report" 2014). To counter, the tobacco industry framed it as a business versus a moral issue. Big Tobacco encouraged reporters to interview southern businessmen lamenting the loss of their jobs. The anti-smoking movement responded by encouraging priests to speak out on the "immortality" of telling young children to "act like men" by smoking.

A War of Words

By the 1970s, the cigarette industry moved on to other messaging. It was no longer trying to declare through ads which brands were endorsed by doctors, as it had in the 1950s. Now, in the rebellious 1960s and early 1970s, the industry tapped into the anti-authoritarian, individualistic social undercurrent. Cigarettes were marketed as a symbol of defiance to a pointedly defiant generation.

Smoking ads played on the rebellious and notorious connotations of cigarettes. Cigarette ads from Camel, Virginia Slims, and Newport cigarettes used counterculture archetypes to market smoking. The ads tapped into burgeoning movements in women's liberation, sexual freedom, and black power. For example, Virginia Slims, the first-ever brand marketed to women, associated the product with the women's movement, going so far as to use the comic book heroine, Superwoman, in one of its campaigns. The tagline was, "We make Virginia Slims especially for women because they are biologically superior to men." Similarly, Newport cigarettes aimed its commercials at the black community, featuring the radical chic imagery popularized by the Black Panther movement (Elkayam 2013). By linking the public's "right to smoke" with other "rights" of the day—such as civil rights for minorities and equal rights for women—the cigarette industry attempted to position tobacco freedom as yet another of the nation's social movements.

The communication efforts of the antitobacco movement had to adapt to compete with the aspirational tone of the cigarette industry's ads. While smoking ads were defiantly glamorous, the antitobacco effort worked to bring it back to reality. Tobacco control advocates focused on exposing the destructive effects of tobacco on the inside of a smoker's body.

The antitobacco campaign also began to push for restrictions that would ban cigarette ads on television. It invested in campaigns that showed celebrities speaking out against the deceptive marketing tactics and the health hazards of cigarettes. The first antismoking ad produced by the American Cancer Society featured children imitating their smoking parents. It was created in 1961 by political ad guru, Tony Schwartz, who a few years later created the famous "Daisy Ad," credited for helping Lyndon Johnson win the presidency (Fox 2008).

Another ad created by the American Cancer Society in 1967 featured television star, William Talman, best known for his role as Hamilton Burger, the district attorney who perpetually lost to TV's famous lawyer, Perry Mason (on the "Perry Mason Show"). The ad struck a nerve. It intimately depicted the actor playing with his young children and young wife. In a pensive voice he talked about how cigarettes "would take [him] away" from his small children and wife. Four weeks after airing, the actor died of lung cancer ("Blowing Smoke: The Lost Legacy of the Surgeon General's Report" 2014).

In 1964, thanks to the antismoking advocates, the Surgeon General required all tobacco companies to put warning labels on all cigarette packs and cartons. A typical label read,

> "Caution: Cigarette Smoking is Dangerous to Health. It May Cause Death from Cancer and Other Diseases." And, quite specifically, "Smoking Causes Lung Cancer, Heart Disease, Emphysema and May Complicate Pregnancy" (Dumas, Bethany K. "An Analysis of the Adequacy of Federally Mandated Cigarette Package Warnings," New York: Plenum Press Corp., 1990, p. 309–352).

Antismoking materials often featured vulnerable children exposed to harmful secondhand smoke, working to pull the heartstrings of guilt-ridden parents. Restricting tobacco companies from marketing to children directly was always an important part of the antitobacco movement, with hopes to ensure that the next generation would not start smoking. Efforts also focused on educating teens directly about the health risks of smoking—since that was the same demographic tobacco marketers were targeting.

By the 1970s and 1980s, with greater restrictions on cigarette advertising, the tobacco industry fought back with more sophisticated marketing techniques. They sponsored major televised sporting events, their logos appearing on signage for tennis, football golf, soccer, hockey, and basketball. It was impossible to show live-action shots of the field on network television without also showing the cigarette logos. This was an effective way for tobacco companies to promote their brands while staying within the limits of the regulations.

Another blow to Big Tobacco emerged in the 1980s. Research proving the hazards of secondhand smoke posed another challenge to tobacco's messaging. While pro-smoking talking points from the 1970s and 1980s stoked a rallying cry for "smokers' freedom," that right was now infringing on the public's rights to clean air. (See the debate on CSPAN, between John Banzhaf, executive director of Action on Smoking and Health, and Brennan Moran, the assistant to the president at the Tobacco Institute, arguing the rights of smokers and the rights of nonsmokers.) (www.c-span .org/video/?309-1/rights-smokers)

When the Environmental Protection Agency (EPA) enacted the Clean Air Act, smokers could no longer freely impose their will on others ("The health consequences of smoking: 50 years of progress" 2014). The American Lung Association's antismoking materials leveraging the new Act, encouraged nonsmokers to be more vocal to exercise their legal rights to breathe smoke-free air.

In 1970, other federal agencies, such as the Labor Department and its Occupational Safety and Health Administration (OSHA), started becoming involved in the clean air movement. New research proved that airborne carcinogens could be found in secondhand smoke. Thus, OSHA issued regulations to ban smoking in work places (Kluger 1997).

In a massive international effort, the World Health Organization (WHO) introduced "World No Tobacco Day" in 1988—the first-ever program of its kind. The campaign, celebrated every May 31, encourages smokers to abstain from using tobacco for one full day in hopes of helping them quit.

By the 1990s, the public became more supportive of bans on smoking in other public places, including restaurants ("Social Norms and Attitudes About Smoking 1991–2010" 2011) and in the early 2000s, even public parks. Even in the face of continued resistance from the tobacco industry, it appears that the public education campaigns, policy reform, and litigation have worked: attitudes around smoking have turned the tide. But the war is hardly over.

A Winnable War?

The largest cigarette companies in the United States spent $8.37 billion on marketing and $26 million in lobbying efforts in 2011 and 2012 alone ("Legacy Foundation Blog using Tobacco Atlas Stats" n.d.). Yet the number of people in America who smoke have been trending downward dramatically, especially among young people. From 2011 to 2014, the share of American high school students who smoked traditional cigarettes declined substantially, from 16 to 9 percent (Tavernise 2015).

The Washington, DC-based American Legacy Foundation is the nation's largest public health foundation devoted to tobacco use, prevention, and cessation. It has introduced several successful public education programs including: *Truth*, a national youth smoking prevention; EX, designed to improve smokers' approach to quitting; and several research initiatives, set out to explore the causes of smoking and most effective approaches to quitting. Its creation came about as a result of the Master Settlement Agreement (MSA) reached in 1988 by attorneys general from 46 states, five U.S. territories, as well as the tobacco industry. The organization uses market intelligence, government outreach, and unique public relations programs to curb tobacco usage. It bases its tactics on information found inside tobacco companies' annual reports, as well as in the troves of documents made public by the tobacco settlement. To encourage the public to access these documents, it established the Legacy Tobacco Documents Library, an online resource, at the University of California, San Francisco.

Legacy employs Ketchum as its public relations agency of record, with messaging and media geared to Millennial and Gen Z audiences (Bradley and Nichols 2014). Born between 1980 and 2001, Millennials account for 31 percent of the U.S. population, outpacing members of Gen X (born 1965–1979) and Boomers (1946–1964). According to Morrison (2003), Millennials:

- Are civic minded and socially aware.
- Feel compelled to make the world a better place.
- Value being good people over career and even marital success.
- Value brands that show the ability to change with consumer feedback.
- Would rather spend on a desirable experience than on coveted gadgets.

And, they rely on social media to consume information and vet brands:

- 60 percent of Millennials said social media was the foremost way they are influenced by brands. Only 31 percent claimed print media was (Horowitz 2014).

The current *Truth* campaign ads run on MTV, VH1, and Bravo, all of which have relatively high ratings of the target. Since Millennials are known to be wary of overt marketing tactics, the ads tap into their savvy and cynicism. One of the ads calls out certain celebrities who inadvertently make cigarettes appealing to young people, with a plea to the generation to "end smoking now."

The ads are also designed to appeal visually to Millennials, incorporating aesthetic trends used to promote music and technology. *Truth* is also seen on laptop, mobile phone, and TV screens with electronic music, streaming texts and an ethos that some characterize as similar to "Occupy Wall Street." The ads frame smoking as a curable epidemic that Millennials can defeat—a message likely to resonate with a civic minded, socially active generation.

But not everyone in the demographic is able to be convinced. In an April 15, 2015, interview with the author, Robin Koval noted that "People with the most education and access to cessation tools are the people who have stopped smoking. Smoking has become a behavior that is more concentrated in lower socioeconomic groups."

The challenge, says Robin Koval, Legacy CEO, is knowing how to reach this new generation. "The way we can message to people has changed a lot," said Koval. "We don't have to exclusively use mass approaches anymore. Through digital tools, we have the ability to tailor messages and reach folks that we never have before." An example is Legacy's work with the Lesbian Gay Bisexual Transgender (LGBT) community, a demographic long targeted by the tobacco industry. The Foundation has used publicity to show this group how Big Tobacco profits from them and also provides the community resources to help them quit.

"Media has changed so much," said Koval. "We think there's an opportunity to use the power of this generation, their social influence and peer-to-peer influencing." And Koval thinks these efforts are also sending a message to Big Tobacco.

> The facts are, if you look at what public health and tobacco control efforts can do—decrease prevalence dramatically, and what we have done that with public education programs, clean air laws and [increased] pricing—it's a winnable battle," she said. "The tobacco industry knows that well. If you look at where they are focusing their efforts—it's not hard to see the United States isn't a growth market—they're focused on outside the United States where tobacco control isn't as advanced as it is here.
>
> And that's where Big Tobacco is headed next.

The Battleground Moves Overseas

Smoking rates in the United States have declined steadily since the 1960s. Internationally, there are countries doing more to fight big tobacco than ever. But there is a long way to go.

The tobacco industry is ramping up its use of international trade agreements to slow health education gains made by countries around the world. Since 2010, Uruguay has been fighting a legal challenge by Philip Morris International against the country's graphic health warnings on tobacco products. The challenge is being funded in part by Bloomberg Philanthropies and international tobacco control advocates. Australia is currently fending off both a World Trade Organization (WTO) challenge and a legal challenge by Philip Morris International against the country's law requiring cigarette packs to be sold in drab colors with very graphic health warnings. It is Australia's tobacco control policy, referred to as "plain packaging." Numerous other countries have also been threatened by the tobacco industry. It is a tactic that can lead to delays by governments in passing and implementing the Framework Convention on Tobacco Control (FCTC)—the world's first-ever health treaty. It has been adopted by more than 180 countries globally ("Bloomberg Philanthropies & The Bill & Melinda Gates Foundation Launch Anti-Tobacco Trade Litigation Fund" 2015).

Conclusion

In the ongoing fight against tobacco, public relations will continue to play a vital role to ensure the tobacco industry is transparent with the public about its manufacturing and marketing practices. The need to change attitudes toward smoking around the world, safeguard the gains made domestically, and protect health will not cease until the war on tobacco is won.

By studying both the tobacco industry's marketing tactics and the strategies that have been used to counter those messages, future public relations may be able to do even more to prevent and curb the harmful effects of cigarettes. Just as the industry has continued to innovate with products like electronic cigarettes, and has expanded into new markets overseas, the public relations strategies used to keep the tobacco industry in check must also evolve. From crafting messages that resonate with new generations, to using new digital platforms to reach them, the public may well one day to win "The War on Tobacco."

Takeaway

Edward Bernays, the public relations pioneer responsible for the 1929 "Torches of Freedom" campaign, was the first in a long line of communicators and marketers to advise cigarette companies how to persuade more women to smoke. But in 1964, after the release of findings proving connections between tobacco and cancer, the Surgeon General called Bernays directly, asking for help to undo the damage caused by 45 years of cigarette promotion.

Bernays turned directly to public relations firms with pleas to sever their ties with tobacco companies. He tried to play on their guilt and shame, admitting his own. Many of the firms, however, countered that everyone had the right to be represented. The cigarette companies were, after all, some of their largest clients.

Bernays would later lament that it was far easier to promote smoking than it was to stop it. Sadly, his own wife, Doris' smoking habit contributed to her fatal stroke in 1980.

As shown in this chapter, the Legacy Foundation's War and Tobacco has succeeded in large part because of its creation of specific messaging for specific audiences. Thanks to social media, it can zero in on certain demographics, such as the various segments within the LBGT market, with emotional appeals backed by statistics.

The growing success of the antitobacco movement proves the value of deploying customized campaigns to effect behavioral change in specific audiences. Mass media appeals are no match for highly targeted campaigns, especially when it comes to the highly cynical audience of Millennials. Finally, the cigarette marketers are losing the battle.

Against seemingly impossible odds, outspent and outgunned by Big Tobacco, the movement has fueled enormous social change in America. Now the battlefield has moved to emerging markets. Again the competition from the tobacco companies will be daunting, and the communications challenges even greater. It will take continued commitment and resources to continue the fight and hopefully to continue the success.

CHAPTER 6

The Campaign for Tobacco-Free Kids

"C'mon, take a drag . . ." Kids have been hearing this from their peers for decades. Smoking is cool. Smoking is adult. Smoking is rebellious. Smoking makes you part of the in crowd.

For the under-18 population—one especially vulnerable to outside influences from peers, TV, movies, advertising, and the Internet—antismoking communication efforts have experienced mixed success globally. While fewer youth are smoking today, the number is still high enough to warrant concern and action, especially when up against a tobacco industry that has so much profit to gain with each new young smoker.

The fight against youth smoking has employed an ongoing variety of different public relations and communication approaches over the years. Governments and nonprofit organizations have spent billions of dollars attempting to convince kids of the dangers of smoking, urging them to never start or continue. These include marketing communications campaigns, social and school programs, and even fundraising walks. Public relations have played an instrumental role in all of those efforts.

Much progress has been made in the fight against smoking in kids in America. Youth smoking has declined from a high 42 percent in 1965 to 18 percent in 2012 ("The Health Consequences of Smoking" 2014). Overall opinions on smoking have changed drastically, from generally favorable to one that recognizes its serious negative impacts on health. Many municipalities, the largest being New York City, have even gone so far as to ban or severely restrict smoking in public areas.

Despite all these efforts, the use of tobacco in the United States, as reported in the U.S. Department of Health and Human Services Surgeon General Report (2014) is still the single largest preventable cause of premature death and disease. Cigarette smoking kills approximately 480,000 Americans each year, including more than 41,000 nonsmoking adults from exposure to secondhand smoke. In addition, smoking-related illness in the United States costs up to an estimated $333 billion a year, including nearly $176 billion for direct medical care of adults and $151 billion in lost productivity due to premature death. According to the U.S. Department of Health and Human Services (2014), every day more than 3,200 U.S. kids under the age of 18 start smoking. Moreover, nearly 9 out of 10 smokers in the United States start smoking before the age of 18, clearly highlighting the importance of targeting this group. If we remained complacent and no further action was taken to reduce the current rates of smoking, in 2014 Surgeon General Report estimated that 5.6 million children under the age of 18 alive today would eventually die prematurely from smoking-related illness.

While there have been several communication and public relations campaigns to underscore the menace of kids smoking, very few stand out for their consistent and dogged efforts in the fight. While governmental organizations and nonprofits have invested billions of dollars in communicating against kids smoking, their efforts have not been sustained and have produced mixed results.

The "Campaign for Tobacco-Free Kids" is a notable exception—relentlessly advocating policies that discourage kids' smoking. Public relations leader Bill Novelli, founder of the global public relations firm Porter Novelli, is the organization's past president and current board chair. The Campaign states their mandate as promote, expose, strengthen, mobilize, empower, and inform public policy makers, organizations, and youths on stop-smoking programs, and drive tough regulations of tobacco products and their marketing (www.tobaccofreekids.org/who_we_are/).

Established in 1996, the Campaign focuses on issues and latest initiatives on the fight to curb tobacco use in the United States and around the world. It has a dedicated media center, which features press releases, recent developments, and updates from various government agencies and organizations working together to stop tobacco use and save lives.

Matthew Myers, current president of the organization, stated in his 2014 annual report that The Campaign for Tobacco-Free Kids offers "proven solutions to save lives and win the fight against tobacco" (www.tobaccofreekids.org/who_we_are/annual_reports/).The organization has established partnerships worldwide with foundations like the Bill and Melinda Gates foundation to further its cause of fighting tobacco use in kids.

Over the course of nearly 20 years, the Campaign has used a variety of public relations, lobbying and advertising techniques to tackle this enormous challenge. For instance, it created Kick Butts Day in 1995. This day is intended to empower youth to stand out, speak up, and seize control against Big Tobacco. Kick Butts Day now includes more than 1,000 events planned by independent organizers across the United States and around the world. It also created a program aimed at school supply retailers urging them to discontinue the sale of cigarettes in stores where children shop.

Each year the Campaign for Tobacco-Free Kids honors the accomplishments of outstanding young people who are among today's most effective leaders in tobacco control. Youth Advocates have worked to promote tobacco prevention at the local, state, national, and international level. Their achievements are celebrated each spring before an audience of more than 500 business, philanthropic, and government leaders.

Lobbying

The Campaign led the fight for a new law, passed by Congress and signed by President Obama in 2009, giving the Food and Drug Administration (FDA) authority to regulate tobacco products and marketing. The Obama Administration also launched the first national tobacco control strategy, which calls for a public education campaign and other actions to prevent kids from smoking. The Campaign works at the state and local level too, on programs and regulations that can reduce the toll of smoking on kids. These efforts include higher tobacco taxes, strong smoke-free laws in all workplaces and public spaces, and well-funded, sustained tobacco prevention and cessation programs.

Recently, the Campaign introduced a new strategy, working with local communities and states to increase the minimum legal sale age for tobacco products to 21. On June 19, 2015, Hawaii became the first state to raise the tobacco sale age to 21. At least 80 localities in eight states, including New

York City, have also raised the tobacco sale age to 21. Statewide legislation to do so is also being considered in several states, including California.

The Media Center

Perhaps the most important aspect of The Campaign's organization is its Media Center. It includes an art gallery, fact sheets, and press releases from various federal agencies and local organizations engaged in the "War on Tobacco." A peek at the art gallery clearly shows that one of the group's main objectives is to "hold tobacco companies accountable for their marketing practices and deception" ("Tobacco Free Kids" n.d.). Thus, many of the industry's most effective print ads and marketing campaigns are featured for public and press review in the "Tobacco Industry Ad Gallery."

The Campaign's fact sheets outline the progress to reduce tobacco usage in the United States and globally. Worth noting here is the amount of money spent on tobacco-related advertising and marketing campaigns: some $9.6 billion each year, or more than $26 million each day ("The Toll of Tobacco in the U.S.A." 2016). Also worth noting is the toll of tobacco on kids' health—more than 165,000 children are killed each year from secondhand smoking ("Toll of Tobacco Around the World" n.d.).

The excerpts below from the ("Toll of Tobacco Around the World" n.d.) fact sheet outline the economic toll of tobacco:

- Health care costs associated with tobacco-related illnesses are extremely high. In the United States, annual tobacco-related health care costs amount to US$96 billion; in Germany, US$7 billion; in Australia, US$1 billion.
- Tobacco-related illnesses and premature mortality impose high productivity costs to the economy because of sick workers and those who die prematurely during their working years.
- Lost economic opportunities in highly populated developing countries will be particularly severe as tobacco use is high and growing in those areas.
- Countries that are net importers of tobacco leaf and tobacco products lose millions of dollars a year in foreign exchanges.

- Fire damage and the related costs are significant. In 2000, about 300,000 or 10 percent, of all fire deaths worldwide were caused by smoking. The estimated total cost of fires caused by smoking is more than $27 billion.
- Tobacco production and use damage the environment and divert agricultural land that could be used to grow food.

International Activities

More than 80 percent of smokers around the world live in low- and middle-income countries. The Campaign for Tobacco-Free Kids works internationally in Africa, Asia, Latin America, and Europe, using many of the same techniques that have proven effective in the United States.

Mark Hurley, the Campaign's International Advocacy Director for Indonesia, is at the front lines for tobacco control in a country with some of the highest smoking rates in the world ("New Survey: Indonesia Has Highest Smoking Rate in the World" 2012, September 12). Hurley feels that while there are some tactics and lessons that can be learned from the United States' antitobacco work, the fact is that in low- and middle-income countries, there is a wide gap in cultural attitudes and understanding about the risks of smoking.

> "What we've learned from the U.S. are the elements that go into effective campaigns. You have to do good communications work that gets to the policy [leaders] and the public. You have to mobilize grass roots organizations so that you have a growing voice of people putting pressure on the public policy and you have to be good at direct political advocacy because the tobacco companies are right there with lobbying," he said during an interview with Rebecca Carriero (2015).

But the question remains, how effective can advocacy work be on a limited budget? "A lot of the public messaging is starting to make a change, but the level of public awareness is not at the level it needs to be," continued Hurley.

Hurley said the problem is Big Tobacco has a good reputation in low- and middle-income countries. In many countries, the tobacco industry gives to charity and does a lot of work that governments cannot do. In Indonesia, Hurley noted, the tobacco industry has funded a good deal of disaster relief. The industry even sponsors concerts. While graphic mass media campaigns showing the health impacts of smoking have had a tremendous impact in moving the needle, Hurley went on to say that "preventing tobacco use saves lives, but it's not always the argument that gets you the furthest for policy change."

Tobacco control advocates in low- and middle-income countries, he says, are focused on helping governments understand how tobacco use escalates health care costs, often borne by the government. In some regions of the world, vital resources should be spent on eradicating deadly diseases, like HIV and malaria. With Big Tobacco moving in, the industry is introducing an unnecessary and costly problem into these countries.

Hurley went on to explain,

> "We try to frame tobacco control as a national development issue. Showing how much a country is spending to treat all of the illnesses caused by tobacco use helps show that it's money that should go elsewhere. In places like Africa where there is a huge burden of treating HIV and Malaria, they should drive down rates of tobacco use because it's easy to do and it's costing money."

Framing the health issue as a *fiscal issue* resonates with policy leaders, he says. "If you can raise [tobacco] taxes, you can raise tens of millions of dollars for your national budget. It's a win–win because it's a public and fiscal issue."

An Assessment

Beyond the efforts of nonprofit organizations and governments, the fight against tobacco use by kids has been made hugely popular by the media and the media has been instrumental in the fight. But it continues to contribute to the problem by including tobacco advertising, much needed revenue in today's media environment.

In June 2015, *The New York Times* published a controversial story that exposed the U.S. Chamber of Commerce's campaign against antismoking laws globally. Responding to the article, Matthew L. Myers,

President, Campaign for Tobacco-Free Kids, noted that the Chamber of Commerce is the "tobacco industry's most formidable front group." The story also disclosed that a "top executive at the tobacco giant Altria Group serves on the chamber's board" ("U.S. Chamber of Commerce Works Globally to Fight Anti-Smoking Measures" 2015). Media stories are important in underscoring the progress and problems still encountered in the long-standing campaign to keep kids from smoking. If large organizations like the U.S. Chamber of Commerce are engaged in practices aimed at repealing antitobacco policies around the world, one wonders the extent to which lobbyists can impact the Campaign's progress overseas.

On a brighter side, the pushback on lobbyists and organizations that support tobacco industry has been fierce and relentless. The contributions to candidates from tobacco-growing states and Political Action Committees (PACs) from the tobacco industry have declined since 2002. Corporations like CVS—which have stopped the sale of tobacco products—have even cut ties with the Chamber, explaining that its "lobbying activity ran counter to its mission to improve public health" ("CVS Health Leaves U.S. Chamber of Commerce over Smoking Stance," *The Wall Street Journal*, July 7, 2015).

From a global standpoint, some governments have also condemned the U.S. Chamber's actions. For instance, the Norwegian health minister noted that protecting the interests of the tobacco industry at the cost of people's life and health was unacceptable.

Conclusion

There is no doubt that the behavioral and cultural shifts by individuals, organizations, and governments toward a tobacco-free environment have helped reduce the overall usage of tobacco products in kids. The ongoing efforts of the Campaign for Tobacco-Free Kids stand out as a good example of what can be done with a firm commitment, ongoing effort, and the use of contemporary public relations techniques.

While the traditional media have been instrumental in the fight, it is however worth recognizing that they still benefit from the paid media and sponsorship efforts of Big Tobacco. Countering that, the prevalence of social media promises to balance the scales. The Campaign for Tobacco-Free Kids is proving with its use of contemporary public relations techniques that reducing kids' tobacco use can be accomplished so long as the right influencers and advocates stand behind organizations dedicated to the fight.

Takeaway

It's no surprise that the Campaign for Tobacco-Free Kids would be a model of success in the war on smoking. Bill Novelli, the organization's founder, built one of the world's great public relations firms on a foundation of health education and socially responsible campaigns.

There are particular elements of the campaign that stand out as effective tools in raising awareness about activities of the tobacco industry, and reducing tobacco addiction in underage kids, at least in the United States.

A "Cigarette Ad Gallery" featured on the campaign's website lays bare the pernicious underbelly of cigarette marketing—its clever creative ad messages. A look at the ads reveals how each lays claim to a different demographic. A Benson & Hedges billboard showcases rollerbladers. Newport ads show African American couples in the suburbs. Lucky Strike features cool twenty somethings. Virginia Slims uses models of every race and color. And a Camel ad appeals the nonconformist Millennial generation, commanding, "Say no to saying no."

While the issues management campaign in developed countries focuses mainly on health concerns, in developing countries it wisely frames tobacco use instead as a fiscal issue. Government leaders in poor countries, already dealing with HIV and malaria, have been persuaded to increase the tax on tobacco as a way to curb cigarette use. By doing so, they portray themselves to their citizens as acting in the public's best interests.

Tobacco-Free Kids in the past 20 years has helped dramatically change the attitudes of adolescents in the United States. The real problem is now in the developing world, the last bastion of growth for Big Tobacco.

CHAPTER 7

When Music is the Message

How Reggae Built Understanding for Rastafarianism

Enchanting Calypso melodies can instantly transport a listener to the palm-lined shores of a Caribbean island. But reggae is so much more than just a beat, or a bass line. It is about a socio-religious movement known as *Rastafarianism*, founded some 80 years ago in the slums of Jamaica and made famous by performers like Bob Marley and Matisyahu. It is also a culture, a way of life, that—with its dreadlocks, cannabis, and bright colored clothing—is both mystical and a mystery to those in Western culture.

Instead of using mass media, the Rastafarians have primarily spread their messages through music. Reggae has not only become its medium for communicating; it is its official voice as well. The beat sets the mood, the lyrics tell the story. Together they work to raise awareness for the Rastafarian religion, build positive feelings for Jamaica, and build a positive image for the Rasta culture.

The rebellious image that was initially painted of the movement by the press in the 1960s and 1970s was largely reset by reggae musicians, who helped project a far more multidimensional picture of its followers. Beyond the dreadlocks and marijuana the public saw on the surface, the reggae performers and their music demonstrated the humanistic values that the movement stood for: racial equality, an end to poverty, and a respect for individual spirituality.

This chapter explores how the relationship forged between Rastafarianism and reggae music built understanding for the movement. It also explores how Marcus Garvey, the Jamaican civil rights leader, played a critical role in the founding of the movement. Garvey's broad-based communications efforts, combined with reggae music, created a unique platform for informing and influencing the public. Reggae music is, indeed, a special kind of "public relations."

Reggae: "Jamaican Soul Music"

Musician Alton Ellis dubbed reggae as an "unfinished music"[1] because Jamaica's development itself is "unfinished" (Nagashima 1984, p. 176). The origin of the movement's name is still disputed, though may be derived from the 1967 song, "Do the Reggay" (Davis and Simon 1977, p. 17). Some think reggae derives from the Jamaican slang for "raggedness."

In its earliest form, reggae was slower and used more bass than rock music (Davis and Simon 1977), a fitting vehicle for its moody rants on life, love, and society. "This is why reggae has been regarded as protest music and has functioned as a deputy for the Rastafarian movement." (Nagashima 1984, p.180). Early hits focused on young thugs, common at the time, ("rude boys" or "rudies"), as a way of broadcasting the extent of Jamaica's poverty. A prime example can be seen in Desmond Dekker's 1969 album, *This is Desmond Dekker,* "007 (Shanty Town)":

And now rude boys have a wail
Cause dem out a jail
Rude Boys cannot fail
Cause dem must get bail
Dem a loot, dem a shoot, dem a wail
A shanty town.

[1]Originally from Reggae Hits the Brooklyn Streets. *New York* Magazine, November 4. JAH Rastafari One: Report of 10th Anniversary Issemble.

The Movement's Beginnings: Marcus Garvey

"Progress is the attraction that moves humanity"

Marcus Mosiah Garvey, born August 17, 1887, in Saint Ann, Jamaica, came from a large, poor family. The family's financial challenges drove him at a young age to become a printer's apprentice. As he grew to become a master printer he saw the role politics and civil rights played in the lives of everyday people, and the hardships suffered when workers at the printing company went on strike in 1909. Soon after, Garvey started to tap into his experience and launched a newspaper of his own called *Watchman*. He used the paper to communicate "the prejudices and other adversities for blacks" (Jeans 1998), and supplemented his writings by sharing his beliefs and ideas in speeches to massive crowds in Central and South America.

In 1915, Garvey founded the Universal Negro Improvement Association (UNIA). It provided charitable educational support to improve the lives of people of African ancestry throughout the world, and it widely promote black consciousness. In 1918, he launched a weekly newspaper called *Negro World*, published under the UNIA banner. While the paper mainly covered news events, it also included Garvey's editorials on the front page of every issue.

Responding to increasing violence against blacks in the United States, Garvey wrote more and more on the economic disparities between American whites and blacks. He gained support not only in the United States, but in communities throughout the world. When *The Negro World* launched French and Spanish editions, readership grew to more than 65,000 (Martin 1976).

Garvey ". . . wanted a worldwide confraternity of the Black Race; [he] wished to see the development of Africa from a backward, colonial enclave to a self-supporting giant of which all blacks could be proud. He wanted to see the development of black educational institutions for the teaching of black cultures. And last he wanted to work for the uplifting of the black race anywhere it was to be found" (Barrett 1997, as cited in Jeans 1998, p. 66).

Garvey's tireless campaigning to boost black pride in his newspapers and speechmaking became the foundation of the new Rastafarian movement. It is known that "Much of their religion is directly descended from Garvey's movement, adopting many of his beliefs as well as symbols" (Jeans). Garvey's beliefs and ideals are evident in the lyrics of reggae music to this day.

Rastafarianism—The Religion

"Jah sitteth in Mount Zion, and rules all creation!"

—Bob Marley

Rastafarianism began as a religious movement—promoting such universal messages as liberty, equality, and an end to oppression—years before it became a social movement. Preaching "social change, and reggae as the means of spreading these beliefs" (Spiker), Garvey said the Rastafarian faith was inherent within everyone's soul, awakened largely by means of inspiration, vision, and the like" (Nagashima 1984, p. 17).

The religion sought "freedom from the religious, economic, social and political domination that whites have exercised over blacks since the beginning of the African slave trade" (Gayraud 1984, as cited in Spiker 1998, p. 121). At first, some saw Rastafarianism as the Jamaican version of the U.S. Civil Rights Movement. But over time, as the public became more familiar with it—through writings, rallies and, of course, music—the public came to recognize Rastafarianism for the religion and distinct social movement that it was.

As Rastafarianism became more popular, it created rules of observance that true believers had to uphold. "Many of its tenets are culled from the Old Testament . . ." (Best 1981). While many of its followers, known as *Rastas*, wear their hair in dreadlocks (never trimmed or combed) there are many who never did. However, as the writings state: "you don't have to be dread to be Rasta" (Lyrics from "Don't Haffi Dread" by Jamaican reggae group Morgan Heritage).

Many devotees, while not outwardly appearing to be Rastas, nonetheless share its spiritual beliefs and practice its rituals in other ways. They must be vegan, abstain from alcohol, and "consume massive amounts of strong Jamaican ganja (marijuana), while citing biblical justification for partaking in what they call the bread of life." (Best 1981). In addition, they must believe in and worship the past Ethiopian emperor, "Haile Selassie I, as JAH" (Elias 2015).

Though Rastas worship Emperor Selassie (who ruled Ethiopia from 1930 to 1974), they are still faithful to the Old Testament. Selassie was selected to be their God because, in 1920, Marcus Garvey urged his followers to "look to Africa where a black king shall be crowned, for the day of deliverance" (Finke 1987, p. 1). Thus, in 1930 when Selassie was named emperor, Rasta adherents considered Garvey's words prophetic.

The playing of Nyabinghi music—a form of communal, chanting, and dancing—is also a ritual of the religion. With the "repetitive drum and bass rhythms" (Elias 2013) Nyabinghi is seen as a close musical cousin to reggae.

Rastafarianism: The Social Movement—A Way of Life

"The concept of Rasta is righteousness."

—Peter Tosh

Rastafarianism advocates for the freedom of the Jamaican people, who had been under British colonial rule since 1655. The movement ". . . was the only voice of a powerless peasant class . . . a symbol of the neglect of an educational system which failed to inculcate in the youth a pride in their homeland" (Spiker 2015). For 1930s colonial Jamaica, the Rastafarian movement gave hope that the oppressed population could one day come out from under its centuries-long rule. And even though the movement strived for a peaceful resolution, it still had to struggle against the politics and ideologies of the day.

Moreover, despite the Rastafarians' campaign to be recognized as a peaceful group, Jamaican society still harbored misconceptions about them. Over time, the upper classes referred to them as dirty, violent outcasts, law-breakers, and antisocial. The movement's leaders fought hard to combat the stereotypes.

Even 30 years later, the University College of the West Indies (now known as University of the West Indies—Mona) published a report describing Rastafarians in this negative light. Rasta leaders demanded that the authors "correct the untrue image and clarify the reality by academic research" (Nagashima 1984, p. 23). Scholars, like Roy Augier, Rex Nettleford, and M.G. Smith (as cited in Nagashima 1984, p. 23), heard the cries of the Rastas and challenged the negative descriptions through new research. They were able to publish their findings in a well-read Jamaican newspaper—*The Daily Gleaner*—with commentary by the Jamaican Premier, Norman Manley. The publication of the academic research helped to disprove common misperceptions of the religion, and did much to change the stereotype of the Rastafarians. The articles produced much discussion in the public, in both black and white Jamaicans. Perhaps most importantly, the articles boosted the morale of the Rastafarian followers and strengthened their resolve.

But soon after the publication of the findings, the group found itself at odds with the Jamaican police. In much of the world, April 12, 1963, was celebrated as Good Friday. But In Montego Bay, thanks to multiple police clashes with Rastas, it became known as "Bad Friday." Police captured and tortured hundreds of Rastafarians. The newspaper *The Gleaner,* painted a portrait of "a gang of Rastafarians, armed with machetes and daggers [who] launched a Holy Thursday rampage that left eight men dead" ("Not much has changed since Coral Gardens incident" The Gleaner, April 7, 1963). Many conflicting reports emerged about the true nature of the events. But the image of the Rastafarians was badly damaged that day.

Even in the years after winning independence from Britain, Jamaica was marred by continued police skirmishes with the Rastas, which further contributed to their negative image. A newly free Jamaica was trying to find its footing in the world—economically, socially, and politically. The movement tried hard to stay away from the "politricks" of the time. But they felt "hostility and ambivalence toward Babylon, the name Rastas gave to what they saw as an oppressive government" (King and Foster 2013, p. 251).

While the Rastafarians began as an apolitical movement, they found, like many of the movements of the Sixties in America, that they were driven to a more political orientation. They were, in part, responding to Haile Selassie's belief that the Rastafarians should be freed from Jamaica and returned to their African homeland. Their political activism was also fueled by the Black Power movement in the United States at the time.

The Rasta movement protested the campaigns of the two Jamaican political parties that had emerged once it became an independent country. They complained that both The Peoples National Party (PNP) and The Jamaica Labour Party (JLP) ignored the movement in the country's first-ever election campaigns in 1967. None of the campaigns promotional materials or advertising reflected Rastafarian culture or used reggae music. Neither campaign leader used references to Rastafarian culture in their political rhetoric.

But this all changed in the 1972 elections. The PNP used both reggae music and images of Rastafarian culture to reach out to the "disaffected youth [while] exploiting the rising popularity of Rastafari" (King and Foster 2013, p. 250). Reggae artists such as Clancy Eccles created songs to win public favor for the PNP. This "musical messaging" was not only effective as a campaign tool; it was a great source of pride, a real morale booster, for the movement. It brought Rastafarianism back out onto Jamaica's center stage. And it also won the support of Prime Minister Michael Manley, something that gave the movement and its ideologies some much-needed credibility.

After the elections, the Rastafarian Movement Association (RMA) was created to "serve(s) a very important function, organizing the Rastafarians into a powerful group that may eventually affect government policy" (Spiker 1998). Today they would likely be regarded as a lobbyist group or political action committee (PAC). Furthering its desire to build bridges with the public, the RMA published a monthly paper. It covered news about the movement in a way that could appeal to a mainstream audience.

The Challenges of Fame

"If you are the big tree, let me tell you that. We are the small axe, sharp and ready..."

—Bob Marley

"Reggae evokes a message of universal suffrage, and in doing so spreads a theme of class consciousness of the poor, illiterate, and oppressed" (Spiker 1998). The emotional power of the music provokes outrage at the conditions of the Jamaican people, and does so in the most far-flung corners of the world. Early reggae artists showed, through their music, the sufferings of the people of Jamaica." (Spiker 1998)

With the music's broad appeal, it took no time for record companies to market reggae internationally and to turn its performers into stars. While ardent adherents would condemn the idea of profiting from a sacred religion, few could turn away the chance to get the Rastafarian messages out into the mainstream, particularly in Europe and North America. To boost popularity of some of the recordings, audio producers would "supervise the overdubbing of flowing guitar lines by British session men and remixed the tracks so that the bass-heavy sound would be more palatable to British and American kids" (Davis and Simon 1997, p. 35).

As the music began to rise in the charts, so did the number of teens—in Jamaica as well as the United States—who began to imitate the ways of the Rastas, growing their hair into dreadlocks, and practicing other the movement's less legal tenets. They wore tee shirts proclaiming, "Legalize it" and hoodies featuring photos of Bob Marley. At the same time, scholars around the world began studying the religion and its impact on Western culture, publishing papers that lent the movement previously unattainable intellectual legitimacy.

Reggae music, still high in the charts, has for the last few decades managed to spread the message of the movement to millions across Europe and America. Most listeners, it is fair to say, have some idea of what the songs try to communicate, and a fair number understand the socioeconomic issues the lyrics try to expose.

At the same time, a new generation of Rasta musicians takes more seriously the responsibility that comes with being the "face" of the Rastafarian religion. Artists including Chronixx, Protoje, and Matisyahu (who was born an orthodox Jew) are actively seeking interviews, TV appearances, and, naturally, social media to give voice to the fundamentals of the religion. As Matisyahu explained his role to *The Guardian*: "we are modernizing reggae staples and breathing new life into the roots of the reggae movement" (The Guardian. Online Interview 2013). In an interview with MTV (2013), he claimed that his message is all about spreading the belief system of Rastafari:

> "We're trying to reach the people. We want to tell them that Rastafari is the way and it's worked for millions of people around the world. It doesn't preach the negativity or carelessness or anything that is harmful to humanity. But it does preach a healthy and righteous life style—pure heart, clean heart."

By phrasing the Rastafarian philosophy in such an easy-to-understand, compelling way—and demonstrating how the religion is relevant to young people today—the new reggae artists hope to build awareness for

Rastafarianism to a new generation. To make Marcus Garvey's goals a reality these young artists communicate—not only through music—but through the practice of tried-and-true media relations as well. While the roots of the religion are complex and not obviously relevant to today's generation, the overall goal of the religion remains fulfillment, a theme that appeals to all young people.

Conclusion

Judging the campaign on how well it created *awareness* for the movement, using reggae as its strategic communication vehicle, the campaign should be considered very effective.

On the other hand, the effort to build *understanding* for the Rastafarian movement or religion, was less successful. While millions of young people may seem to have embraced the Rasta culture—its practices, rituals, and appearance—the true meaning behind the religion has not been connected with the millions of reggae fans. It is easy to look and act like a Rasta; but embracing its complex belief systems and political undertones are not the stuff that generally interests the fans of its music.

Some of the blame may fall to pop culture, where Rastas continue to be portrayed in films, television, and media coverage as dreadlocked potheads in crocheted Rasta hats. Thanks in part to this stereotype, the "Rasta look" has devolved into a sort-of fashion, creating a multimillion-dollar industry worldwide. A Google search turns up nearly 600,000 results for "Rasta clothing." Some of the blame may also fall to the leaders of the movement—or even the performers themselves—for not communicating deeply enough the meaning behind the movement, falling prey perhaps, to the promise of fame and profits. There has been much money made in the commercialization of the Rasta movement since the 1980s.

Takeaway

With the goals of building awareness and understanding, and a strategy of using music to deliver an emotional and impactful message, Rastafarians have tapped a centuries-old approach to public education. From a public relations perspective, this work uses an insight into the audience's wants and matches those with tactics designed to appeal to them. Both Hinduism and Buddhism have used religious music for thousands of years that imparts values. Christian hymns and Christmas carols educate the young and reinforce the religion's values and stories. And the Baptists certainly use their gospel music to excite and educate their flock.

This technique, using "music as the message" to strike an emotional chord, has been demonstrated to be a formidable means of outreach for social movements beyond religion as well. It creates unity and pride, and rouses the spirit. We identify songs with their causes: "We Shall Overcome" with Civil Rights; "It Don't Mean a Thing" with the Harlem Renaissance; "What Are We Fighting For?" during the Vietnam War protests; and "I Am Woman" during the Women's Rights movement. Time and again, music has proven to be a powerful communications tool.

Such was the case with reggae and the grassroots movement it spawned. The movement's leaders, like Bob Marley, were every bit as much communicators as they were musicians. And the music and the lyrics were public relations tools fueling the movement.

Reggae gave the world its first taste of a proud Jamaican heritage. Finally, people outside the Caribbean could understand the uniqueness of the country and the breadth of the Rastafarian religion. The songs, which painted pictures of poverty and political unrest, persuaded the world to pay attention to the plight of the common man. Even young white people the world over began to identify with, and show support for, the Rasta movement, wearing dreadlocks, smoking ganja, and going vegan.

Would the world have been so moved had the story been communicated through press releases, media interviews, or documentaries? Thanks to reggae, we learn that music can not only spark a social movement, it can serve as powerful communication channel, working as well as, if not better than, any other safe, peaceful means.

CHAPTER 8

Battling the Tide of Public Opinion to Build Support for a Jewish State

"All business in a democratic society begins with public permission and exists by public approval." So said public relations pioneer Arthur Page, AT&T's first vice president of public relations, in the 1930s (www.awpagesociety.com/about/background-history/the-page-philosophy/).

While Page was referring to the phone company back then, the same sentiment can apply to any company, or any country, for that matter. Not only is it critical to build public awareness for the entity, but it is also critical to build public understanding for its raison d'être.

It is a tough challenge for all start-up countries, but none tougher than that of the State of Israel, whose path to independence was fraught with more controversy than any new nation in history. And in a land well-known for its miracles, gaining statehood was perhaps the biggest miracle of them all.

This is a story about a group of believers who managed, despite all odds, to turn the tide of public sentiment in their favor. They did this through a carefully executed campaign—using both reason and emotional appeal—to show how the founding of the state was not just in the best interest of the Jews, but of the entire world.

Background

But why was public opinion—even among its allies—so against the state's creation?

The story begins with the Dreyfus Affair in 1894. (Zollmann 2012) Alfred Dreyfus, a French Army captain, was born to Jewish parents in

Mulhouse, Alsace, on the French border with Germany. As a result of the Franco-Prussian war in 1870 to 1871, the area was ceded to Germany and the Dreyfus family, in order to maintain their French citizenship, moved to Paris (Beitler 2008). In the terms of the day, members of the Dreyfus family were called "assimilated Jews."

Though assimilated, Captain Dreyfus was nonetheless a Jew in a land growing increasingly anti-Semitic. He was arrested and falsely accused of spying, then selling French military secrets to the Germans. The only evidence against him was a piece of paper found in a wastebasket which said, in French, that he was going "to deliver a valuable French artillery manual to the Germans" (Zollman 2012).

Zollman goes on to note that handwriting experts could not find a "definitive link" between Dreyfus' handwriting and the note. But, because Dreyfus was a Jewish man from a town now ruled by Germany, the note was more than enough to provoke widespread claims of spying in France's newspapers. Reporters went wild with the story, to the point of sensationalism, not unlike the "yellow journalism" fervor happening at the same time in America. Story after story questioned Dreyfus' loyalty. As one editor wrote, "Was he, above all, French? German? Or part of an 'international Jewish conspiracy'?" (Zollman 2012).

Dreyfus was convicted by a French secret military court and sentenced to life imprisonment on Devil's Island, a penal colony located off the coast of South Africa ("Anti-Semitism" 2015). Zollman notes that this added fuel to the flames of anti-Semitism now sweeping more vigorously across France, military officers stripped him of his rank in a very public, very well publicized disgracing ceremony. French newspapers, such as the right wing *La Libre Parole* used the conviction "as further evidence of Jewish treachery." Its publisher, Édouard Drumont, wrote that "every catastrophe that had befallen France had Jews behind it (Brustein 2003, p. 120)."

Drumont's articles of the 1890s are believed to have been the catalyst behind anti-Semitic movements that started popping up throughout France. According to Brustein (2003, p. 120) a few of the notable ones were *La Ligue antisemitque francaise, L'Union nationale*, and *La Jeunesse antisemite et nationaliste.* These movements captured the attention of a growing number of influential reporters throughout Europe. In the midst of the anti-Semitic frenzy public sentiment began to turning increasingly against the Jews in both Germany and France.

Two years after the Dreyfus conviction officials discovered a new traitorous note, appearing to be in the same hand as the one that convicted him. Since he was locked up in a penal colony, it was impossible for Dreyfus to have written it. Handwriting experts this time traced the note to a military officer, Walter Esterhazy. But despite all the evidence against him, Esterhazy was acquitted. After all, the court said, he was not a Jew, he was one of "their own," and thus was protected by the State.

After this, Dreyfus was granted a retrial. Though the courts found him guilty again, Zollman notes that he was given a reduced sentence, because of "extenuating circumstances." As news of the new verdict spread across Europe, it ignited a public outcry. Bowing to public pressure, the liberal President of France, Emile Loubet, eventually pardoned Dreyfus in 1899.

The "Dreyfus Affair" now headline news throughout the Continent, struck fear in Jews throughout Europe. Here was Dreyfus, a man who seemed to be a completely "assimilated Jew," but nonetheless was still regarded by his homeland as an "outsider." What could this mean for other "assimilated" Jews in Europe?

It was during these fearful days that the idea for forming a Jewish state—known as the Zionist movement—took hold in the mind of French Jew named Theodor Herzl.

The Birth of Zionism

As reported in *A Brief History of Israel* (Reich 2008), a Viennese daily, *Neue Freie Presse* sent a young Paris correspondent to cover the Dreyfus scandal. As Theodor Herzl reported on the trial he could feel the anti-Semitic fervor escalating around him. Perhaps the best solution—for Jews and non-Jews—was to found a homeland for the Jewish people. He made his case for Zionism in a pamphlet called, *Der Judenstaat* (The Jewish State 1896). After the booklet's publication, Herzl traveled by horse and carriage around the continent to publicize his ideas and gain support for the cause from Jews and non-Jews alike. Modern public relations would call that a "road show" or a "media tour."

Herzl's message was "we are people, one people. We recognize ourselves as a nation by our faith" (Friedman 2004, p. 47). Reich (2008, p. 16) notes that he viewed anti-Semitism as a "phenomenon that appeared wherever Jews were located." Herzl believed the Jewish people needed their own nation, and that the nations that vilified Jews would support a Jewish homeland. After all, the Jews would now be out of their hands. Herzl debated between two locations for his vision, Argentina and Palestine, with the preferred location in Palestine.

The Zionist movement officially began in 1897 with the World Zionist Congress, convened by Herzl in Switzerland. It was there that the "Jewish national movement was formed with the goal of establishing a home in Palestine for the Jewish people" (Friedman 2004, p. 47).

The Jewish Migration

The first wave of immigration to Palestine came from Eastern Europe in 1880s, but the desire to leave was not expressed within "leadership and wealthier segments of the Western [European] Jewish communities" (Reich 2008, p. 15). The early years of the 20th century saw the second wave of immigration, beginning in 1904 and lasting until 1914, the start of the Great War. The Jews now residing in Palestine grew from 25,000 to 85,000.

During that same year, as part of war effort, the British invaded [Palestine] in 1917 seizing control from the Ottoman Empire, which had governed the country since 1517. By 1916 the British presented Palestine to the world as the home for the Jewish people.

Making it Official

During World War I, the Zionist movement continued to grow in strength and influence in the region. Dr. Chaim Weizmann, a Russian Jewish immigrant from Great Britain, and the man who would be elected Israel's first president, orchestrated the issuance of the Balfour Declaration of 1917, guaranteeing that Palestine would be the official homeland for the Jewish people.

Publicized in newspapers around the world, The Balfour Declaration provided the Zionist movement with widespread recognition for their goal and laid the groundwork for the establishment of the Jewish state.

In 1922, both U.S. President Woodrow Wilson and the U.S. Congress endorsed, the Balfour Declaration, driving newspaper and radio coverage across the world.

In 1921 the first of the Arab Riots broke out in Palestine. That led to the creation of the 1922 Churchill White Paper, and its setting immigration quotas for both Jews and Arabs. The Paper stated that no amendments could be made to the Balfour Declaration and that the Jews had the right to be in Palestine ("Jewish Palestine Mandate" 2015, May 4). The immigration quota made way for the third, fourth, and fifth migration to Palestine. By the mid-1920s, nearly one million new Jews had arrived.

These new immigrants represented a cross-section of Jewish society—from academics and artists, to tradesmen and shop owners. With their arrival in Palestine, agriculture, culture, and commerce grew. The Hebrew language also became one of the three official languages of the area, along with Arabic and English.

Next, in 1922, the Council of the League of Nations approved the British mandate for Palestine, which became official on September 29, 1923. The mandate called for the Jews and Arabs living in Palestine to prepare for self-government (McTague 1980). It was during this time that the Jewish community created many of its governing and social support institutions.

One of these institutions was the Jewish Agency (JA), created to facilitate the immigration and settlement of Jews into Palestine. At the same time the Palestinians created the Arab Higher Committee (AHC) a group that represented the various Arab factions (Morris 2008). The AHC wanted the end of the British mandate and Palestinian Independence under Arab rule. As the Jewish population of Palestine grew, so did tension and conflict with the Arabs, who felt Palestine was their homeland as well.

World War II

When Adolf Hitler and the Nazi regime came to power in Germany they waged a relentless propaganda campaign to build even greater hostility against the Jews of Europe. Reich (2008, p. 34) notes that Hitler's plan was to "liquidate the European Jewish community" and to create a true, pure Aryan race. The Holocaust eventually took the lives of more than six million Jews, virtually wiping out 2000 years of European Jewry.

By the end of the war, most Jewish survivors had lost their families, their homes, their jobs, essentially all their worldly goods. Where were they to go now? Media relations campaigns waged by the Jewish aid groups, newspapers, radio, and newsreels urged them to seek refuge in what was now their official homeland—Palestine.

But there was a problem. The British immigration quotas were far smaller than the number of Jews displaced by the war. As a result, many Jews became refugees, and the Zionist cause needed help. They found it in the work of the JA.

The Jewish Agency and Propaganda

Working with the JA, the international press—including newsreels, radio, and print—gave daily coverage of the plight of the displaced Jewish refugees. As the internationally recognized, official mouthpiece of the Zionist movement, the JA led the effort in garnering western media support for the Zionist cause (Goodman 2011).

From the very beginning of its public relations operation, the JA used sophisticated media relations to garner political and financial support from the wealthy elite—both Jews and non-Jews. In 1934, the JA founded its own news agency, the "Palestine Correspondence Agency," known simply as Palcor (Goodman 2011). After the outbreak of World War II the JA established a special department, the Hasbara, to disseminate positive stories. Led by Isaiah Klinov, a former journalist for the daily newspaper, *Ha'aretz* and supervised by the JA's political department (Ben-Shalom 2014), the Hasbara provided ready-to-print press materials to media stationed in Palestine, Europe, the United States, and around the world.

The JA worked with reporters to build greater understanding for the Zionist cause. It gave reporters close-up, high-level access to watch and write personal accounts of refugee efforts to reach Palestine's shores. For instance, JA brought a Pro-Zionist Reuters reporter, Jon Kimche, to witness a successful disembarkation of Holocaust survivors "in the dark of night on a deserted beach near Nahariya in the north of Palestine" in 1945 (Goodman 2011, p. 4). His dramatic, first-person observations of a refugee transport were printed widely in the British press, producing sympathetic responses around the world.

Supporting the JA's press relations strategies was the Haganah, the Jewish paramilitary organization that later became the core of the Israeli Defense Forces. They printed their own dramatic refugee stories in pamphlets, and distributed them to the press worldwide. Haganah also ran its own 10-minute daily radio broadcast, Voice of Israel, which was often quoted in the *Anglo-American Press*. Newspapers like *Hebrew Press* and the *Palestine Post* also served as assets to the JA campaign, furnishing the foreign press with information favorable to the refugee cause.

The Ship that Launched a Nation

The cultivation of the Zionist movement and the fight for a Jewish state all came together in 1947. A ship named the Exodus, acquired by the Haganah, set sailed for Marseille, France on July 11, 1947. On the ship were 4,500 refugees, including 655 children ("Exodus 1947" 2015). These passengers were survivors who came from the ashes of the Holocaust with nowhere else in the world to go.

Their voyage aboard the Exodus lasted seven days. As the ship approached the port city of Haifa, just miles from the Palestine shore, the British Navy abruptly boarded the deck, preventing the refugees from entering the country. Hundreds of the passengers rebelled. Three people were killed, including one crewmember, and dozens were injured. The British took control of the ship and brought it to port.

Journalists and cameramen were standing by as the exhausted passengers disembarked. Reporters aired live play-by-play broadcasts to radio stations around the world. Photographers and film producers recorded dozens of dramatic, heart-wrenching images, absorbed by an international audience over the next few days. The world's leading journalists covered the Exodus story, as well, with moving, first-person accounts sent over the wire services and published by papers around the globe.

Most of the accounts, photos, and films showed hundreds of bedraggled, malnourished people who had (miraculously) survived the death camps. Now, as the world looked on, they were once again being attacked, hurt, and gathered up to be sent away (Trescott 2007). People around the world watched these events unfold day after day.

Prior to the Exodus incident, the British had been sending illegal Palestinian immigrants to detention centers in Cyprus. But to discourage others planning to immigrate to Palestine they loaded the Exodus passengers onto three ships and sent back them to Marseille, France. Once there, the women and children disembarked, but the men refused. They remained on the ship for two months living in deplorable conditions ("Exodus 1947" 2014, June 14).

Eventually on August 22, 1947, the ship sailed for the port of Hamburg, where passengers were forcibly taken off and transported to two camps near Lubeck, Germany. Fortunately, the JA made sure journalists were there to witness the events firsthand. Their reports caused panic across the world.

When photos of the refugees—again surrounded by barbed wire—surfaced in the newspapers and newsreels, the public was outraged. Were the Jews being forced by the British back into concentration camps? Hundreds of protests sprang up around the world, in Europe, Palestine, and the United States. This was surely not the public reaction the British planned on.

The Jews captured the world's sympathy, while the British were the target of scorn and shame. It was a public relations battle the United Kingdom could never win. To resolve the issue, the British government handed over "the question of Palestine" to the United Nations ("War, Peace, & Politics: UN Partition Plan" 2015). The United Nations appointed a Special Committee on Palestine (UNSCOP) to handle the situation. After three months of investigation and hearings in 1947 (Haron 1980, p. 178) they created the Partition Resolution of 1947 (UN General Assembly Resolution 181, as cited in Nasrallah 2011). The Resolution, passed on November 29, 1947, recommended that Palestine be divided into both a Jewish and an Arab state, with Jerusalem and Bethlehem remaining neutral, and under international trusteeship.

The UN vote, carried live to anxious listeners around the world, was one of the first politically significant activities by the newly created body. Millions listened as each member country was called on to voice their vote for or against granting statehood status to Palestine. In living rooms and parlors in every country that broadcast radio could reach, listeners kept track as each "yay," "nay," or abstention was cast. The final tally at the General Assembly: 33 countries voted in favor, 13 against, and 10 abstaining. Against all odds, the State of Israel was born (Haron 1980, p. 178).

On May 14, 1948, one day before the British mandate was set to expire, Israel declared its independence. The Zionist movement, a dream of one lone reporter in France, finally achieved what the world thought impossible. The Jewish people now finally had a country where they could live free from anti-Semitism.

Conclusion

Public relations strategies and tactics played an enormous role in the creation of the Jewish State. From the sensationalist press coverage of the Dreyfus Affair, through the crisis of the Exodus, communications galvanized public opinion, created the Zionist Movement, and kept the issue alive.

This chapter shows the strong links between behavior and communication in making an emotional connection to the public. No doubt, had a contemporary public relations expert been present when the Exodus docked at Haifa, he or she would have warned the British about the reputational damage their behavior would cause, especially with the press there to report firsthand. The "optics" of that incident did not bode well for the British cause; Americans especially, owing to their long-standing friendship with the United Kingdom, felt betrayed and deceived, their trust shaken.

The reporting ignited strong anti-British sentiment around the world. But at the same it made the world finally understand why Israel needed to exist.

Takeaway

The old saying, "a picture is worth a thousand words," remains true for many social movements. The photo of Dr. Martin Luther King, Jr., on the steps of the Lincoln Memorial; the images of young women jumping out of windows at the Triangle Shirtwaist Factory; the nightly TV coverage of Occupy Wall Street all indelibly inscribed themselves in our memories. They can evoke far more powerful emotions than any other device.

But there was one social movement whose images meant life or death for thousands, and became the deciding factor in the fate of a nation. After all, the Zionist movement, which led to the formation of the State of Israel, could not exist without consent of the world community. While the Jewish Agency disseminated many logical reasons for the creation of Israel, the emotion appeal in the form of human-to-human connection finally changed the minds of those most against it, and led to the necessary number of yea votes at the United Nations.

One could be, in principle, anti-Zionist and anti-Semitic. But it is hard for any human being—especially by the end of a war—to sustain those feelings after seeing the skeletal Holocaust survivors denied entry to their "homeland." The Jewish Agency, and the many sympathetic journalists, filmmakers, and photographers it serviced, needed barely a cutline to describe what was happening aboard the Exodus.

Many organizations, brands, and commodities groups use a "news bureau" today to disseminate correct information about their products, services, and ideas. Like modern day news bureaus, the JA was responsible for disseminating news and photos. It used the power of the press to communicate the facts, and turn the tide of public opinion.

What they didn't know at the time was that their work would so quickly turn the tide of public opinion in what was one of the most important events of the 20th century.

This may well be the most powerful media relations story in history.

CHAPTER 9

Feminism from *The Feminine Mystique* to *Lean In*

Sexism in America has a long history. Women were denied the vote by the U.S. Constitution until the Suffragette movement (otherwise known as the "first wave" of the women's rights movement) won passage of the 19th Amendment in 1920. Strong personalities, like Susan B. Anthony, waged a large-scale, sustained public relations campaign that forever changed our laws, culture, and economy.

Since that time, other strong women have championed campaigns that have put discrimination against women in the spotlight and pushed society further in the direction of equal rights for all. This chapter celebrates the lives, and the campaigns of two of them.

Betty Friedan

Betty Friedan was born on February 4, 1921, in Illinois. The daughter of a Jewish immigrant jeweler and a homemaker, she was a highly educated woman in the early 20th century. She graduated *summa cum laude* from Smith College in 1942, and had developed the reputation of being a difficult person because of public scenes she had with men. She played a crucial role orchestrating what is known as the "second wave women's movement," from the 1960s into the 1990s.

In 1966, Friedan went on to found the largest organization in women's movement, called National Organization for Women (NOW). She toured the country advocating for women's rights. Later in her life she focused on issues such as ageism, family issues, and economic empowerment. However, history will always remember her for the role she played in fostering equality for all American women.

The Feminine Mystique

The "first-wave Feminist Movement" began in the 1800s and lasted until 1920. During these decades, women crusaded very publicly to gain the right to vote. Finally, after 70 years of struggle, Congress ratified the 19th Amendment, granting women the right to vote.

The "second wave of the Feminist Movement," following 40 years consumed by Depression and a World War, started percolating in the economic boom years of the 1950s and took off in the civil rights era of the 1960s. Many say the second wave was ignited by a single book more than anything else. That book, Freidan's *The Feminine Mystique*, took society by storm when it was first published in 1963.

The book grew from Friedan's own research into the lives of her former Smith College classmates. She found something particularly interesting, that most of her highly educated peers were unhappy in their roles of housewives. She tried to publish the findings in a periodical, but no magazine wanted to support such a "revolutionary article." Friedan spent the next 5 years developing *The Feminine Mystique* that shaped society in a way few books had before it. The book portrayed the unfulfilling lives these very educated and sophisticated housewives and suburban mothers were now leading. She hoped that with the book, women would reassess their place in the world and eventually maximize their intellectual and economic potential in fulfilling careers.

Friedan, herself a housewife at the time, claimed that suppressed women could not be satisfied conforming to society's "norms," with a husband, two kids, and a house in the suburbs. Self-fulfillment is impossible, she says, by cleaning floors, driving carpools, and keeping the roast warm for her husband. Friedan used her personal narrative to connect to her readers, explaining that she herself gave up the opportunity to pursue a career in psychology in order to comply with society's norms, and raise a family in suburbia.

Friedan revealed that a former boyfriend, intimidated by her success, told her one day that nothing could come of their relationship, because he would never win a fellowship like hers (Friedan 1963). She explained that after making the decision to move to New York, she decided to "live in the present, work on newspapers with no particular plan. I married, had children, lived according to the feminine mystique as a suburban housewife" (Friedan 1963). Thus, Friedan advocated that it is every woman's right to break away from the "feminine mystique" and seek fulfillment in her way. Using anonymous case studies of her Smith classmates, and putting her psychology degree to work on analyzing this demographic, she made a compelling case for women to steer clear of the stereotypes depicted on afternoon commercials and forge her own path, even if that path leads right back to a house in the suburbs instead of a job in the city.

Cultural Climate

Sexist commercials such as the Folgers Coffee campaign in the 1960s portray what life was like for housewives during this period.

The advertising campaign demonstrated the societal pressure women felt trying to please their husbands—and suggested that making them a "decent cup of coffee" for breakfast was a sure way to their hearts. While such a commercial would run counter to today's culture of Type A career women, this was seen as a cultural norm in the early 1960s. Advertisers used market research and focus groups to understand the target's secret desires and disappointments. In the Folgers commercial the desire of the suburban housewife is portrayed to be, above all else, that she should not disappoint her husband. And now, says the commercial, she has the power to keep him happy thanks to a daily dose of Folgers in his cup (www.folgerscoffee.com/about-us/folgers-history.aspx).

The Feminine Mystique was targeted to middle-class white women in post-war suburbia. During the 1960s, the majority of these women were completely dependent on men to provide for them and the kids. Friedan understood that the concept of housework had evolved from farm to suburbia. But unlike their predecessors on the farm, suburban women were not contributing financially to the household. On top of that, the increasingly sophisticated appliances coming onto the market in the 1960s required so little skill that they actually caused housewives to feel even more unfulfilled. Plus, this generation of women generally had children in their early twenties. By the time they were grown up, women in their prime were left empty nested.

The Issue at Hand

As Friedan studied her peers she realized she was not the only one feeling the suppression and suffocation of suburban life. *The Feminine Mystique* opened the door for women to discuss these issues freely with other women. And the more women who spoke out in the open about the issues, the more their feelings became known to the mainstream. More than anything else, *The Feminine Mystique* created the environment for the women's movement to take hold and shape the way the women are viewed. Women felt it was now possible for them to contribute to society in ways that are psychically, intellectually, and economically meaningful to them. And they could still even have that house in the suburbs, although the question of "having it all" would not arise until the turn of the next century.

Friedan was also advocated for "equal pay, sex-neutral help-wanted ads, maternity leave, child-care centers for working parents, legal abortion, and many other topics considered radical in the 1960s and 1970s" (Sullivan 2006). Thanks to the second wave movement, women found the courage to fight against a very biased economic system. They found strength to demand changes to the legal system, so that they could be afforded equal rights to men in every aspect of life.

Friedan founded the NOW in 1966. Using a wide array of public relations techniques, including special events, publicity, speaking engagements, marches, protests, and boycotts, NOW has grown into the largest organization of feminist activists in the United States, with hundreds of thousands of contributing members and more than 500 local and campus affiliates in all 50 states.

NOW has championed the Equal Rights Amendment, prochoice, gender description in the workplace, and admission to the military. Even today, NOW plays a major role bringing a number of critical issues—such as domestic violence and work-family balance—to the forefront of the American agenda.

Sheryl Sandberg and the Modern Day Women's Movement

Sheryl Kara Sandberg, Chief Operational Officer (COO) of Facebook, is a feminist, activist, and author. Born in 1969 in Washington, DC, to a Jewish family, Sandberg graduated from Harvard College *summa cum laude* in 1991. She then went on to enroll in Harvard Business School in 1995 where she earned her MBA. Sandberg is now well known for her role at Facebook and as the creator for the wildly popular "Lean In" movement. To give a sense of the movement's appeal, Sandberg's 2010 TED talk on female leadership secured more than five million views.

"Lean In," is a modern day feminist manifesto published in 2013. The book became an instant sensation and *New York Times* bestseller. The book incited women to *Lean In* to higher professional opportunities. It does this by focusing on three main ideas (1) internalizing the revolution, (2) leaning in, and (3) closing the leadership ambition gap.

By internalizing the revolution, she argued, women can work around their personal obstacles in order to change their mindset and the system. Leaning in refers to women taking action and not holding themselves back professionally. "Only when women finally internalize the revolution, triumph over their internal obstacles and actively lean in to their careers will they be poised to accomplish one of Lean In's key feminist objectives: closing the leadership ambition gap" (Rottenberg 2014, p. 8).

In her book, Sandberg summarizes study after study to inspire readers to get ahead by taking professional risks. For instance, she claims that women only apply to jobs for which they are 100 percent qualified, while men will apply when they are only 60 percent. In her Ted Talk (2010) she explains,

> Women do not negotiate for themselves in the workforce. A study in the last two years of people entering the workforce out of college showed that 57 percent of boys entering, or men, I guess, are negotiating their first salary, and only seven percent of women. And most importantly, men attribute their success to themselves, and women attribute it to other external factors. If you ask men why they did a good job, they'll say, "I'm awesome. Obviously. Why are you even asking?" If you ask women why they did a good job, what they'll say is someone helped them, they got lucky, they worked really hard.

Along with the release of her book, Sandberg launched the "Lean In" Foundation, campaigning against corporate gender inequality. The Foundation describes itself, on its website (Lean In n.d.) this way: "We are committed to offering women the ongoing inspiration and support to help them achieve their goals. If we talk openly about the challenges women face and work together, we can change the trajectory of women and create a better world for everyone."

The Lean In Foundation uses its website to provide a platform for women to share ideas and information. They collect stories from women that chose to "lean in" or "lean back" that are intended to inspire others. They are also building a library of free online lectures on leadership and communication.

Finally, the organization is encouraging women all over the country to start "Lean in Circles," small local groups that meet for encouragement and support. When the book was published, more than 23,000 Circles had been created in 110 countries around the world. According to the organization's website, 75 percent of members credit the Circle with a positive change in their lives.

Importantly, Lean In Circles are not just about business. Circle members report that the organization's philosophy and support have helped them in many aspects of their lives. Some quotes on the website describe how the members' Circles inspired them to. . . .

"Raise my hand more in class and take the lead on group projects."

—Danielle Noel, Washington, D.C., Organizer of Circles at George Washington University

"Lean in to the joys and challenges of being a single mum."

—Vicky McGrath, Dublin, Ireland, Member of Circle called "Ladies of Life Science"

"Help teenage victims of sex trafficking step out of their past and into their future."

—Kathy Andersen, Miami, Florida, Leader of a Circle for sexual abuse victims

Two Generations of Fighting for Change

Betty Friedan's *The Feminine Mystique* and Sheryl Sandberg's Lean In have both used public relations techniques to contribute enormously to the progress women have made, individually, in society and in business.

Both of these leaders set out to enable women to self-fulfillment and transformation. Both urged other women to seek personal satisfaction by pursuing professional goals.

According to Rottenberg (2014), Lean In "tries to identify the source of a recurrent liberal paradox: Given that women's opportunities and progress are no longer obstructed by discriminatory laws and exclusionary institutions, what are the causes of women's continued inequality in the USA?" (p. 7)

While both women targeted a similar demographic of middle class women educated in a host of fields, Sandberg kept her focus on the business world. Although her approach was not intended for every woman, it quickly became clear that all women could benefit from the general message. The general concept of exuding confidence, negotiating for yourself and even finding the right partner are all goals that are consistent within every social economic class.

The success of both of these movements is due, in large part, to basic public relations principals: understanding the needs of their target audience, constructing messages that will resonate with them, delivering them over channels that will influence their attitudes and behavior, and, significantly, employing spokespeople who can deliver the message with clarity, clout, and charisma.

Takeaway

Both Betty Friedan and Sheryl Sandberg built successful campaigns and organizations on key insights into the wants and needs of women at the times of their efforts: the 1960s and 2013. Those insights enabled them to develop messages that resounded with women, and their success was built on that.

Although both women produced important works, Freidan's was considered far more influential, given the culture of the day. In the early 1960s, media and especially advertising consistently depicted images of what women were "supposed" to be doing: mopping the floor at home, driving a carpool in the suburbs, taking dictation in an office. Freidan's bestseller was first to question the stereotypes. Through rallies, TV appearances and newspaper interviews, Freidan's notions—often considered heretical—swept through the nation and radically changed the way society regarded women. More important though, she changed the way women thought of themselves.

Rarely does one book, or one person, affect such changes in society. But the timing was right—it was the rebellious 1960s, after all. Freidan used the power of public relations to spark a cultural awakening like none the nation had ever seen.

As seen in this chapter, both Freidan and Sandberg succeeded because they researched their target markets, understood what made them tick. The power of those audience insights offers a lesson for all communicators. A rich understanding of your audience, whoever it is, is a critical first component in the creation of any successful communications campaign.

CHAPTER 10

The American Civil Rights Movement

The Use of Contemporary Public Relations Techniques by Dr. Martin Luther King, Jr.

In a country that began in civil turmoil, there is perhaps no greater known civil rights advocate in its history than Dr. Martin Luther King, Jr. Renowned for his influence on the Civil Rights Movement of the 1950s and 1960s, Dr. King is honored both for his lifetime contributions and lauded for his heroic peaceful acts for equality in America. King's Christian-based approach to political and civil rights made active use of public relations tools and tactics.

A Baptist minister and learned man, Dr. King's teachings of calm and peaceful resolution were not unlike historical influencers such as Confucius, Gandhi, and Jesus Christ. Following such historic role models, he set out on a journey to change the way 1950s and 1960s America viewed racial injustice and inequality. From his hometown of Atlanta, Georgia, to the streets of Washington, D.C., Dr. King's lasting impact on American culture remains his legacy.

This chapter examines three key events where Dr. King used the power of public relations during the 1950s and 1960s in the American Civil Rights Movement. King's tactics will be shown to cut across racial divides in ways no other civil rights leader has done before or since.

Public relations today works at two levels—influencing the behavior of organizations to align with the public interest and, at the same time, communicating that behavior effectively. This is precisely the approach that Dr. King took to influence the nation's way of thinking about civil rights.

The brilliance behind King's approach was not only his communication, but the way he demonstrated with his own behavior the violence and brutality faced by African Americans through peaceful civil disobedience, "King knew that it would take a combination of action, words, and visibility in the media to eliminate segregation laws and integrate lunch counters, restrooms, water fountains, and businesses" (Hanson 2012). Or, stated differently, the power of public relations.

Dr. King understood the price of that civil disobedience as he built his campaigns. To implement historic change, he knew that he might be risking his own life and the lives of other African Americans in pursuit of total equality. The following three key events will be examined to illustrate King's influence on public relations: The Birmingham, Alabama protest; the March on Washington; and, the Selma to Montgomery March.

King adopted a targeted approach with each event: In Birmingham he focused on violence against African Americans. In Washington he motivated the enormous crowd through rhetoric and emotional appeal. And in Selma he showcased police brutality and racial injustice.

None of these events would have taken place without the founding of the Southern Christian Leadership Conference (SCLC) in 1957. But before that, at the age of 26, King first helped coordinate the famous 1955 Montgomery Bus Boycott. The event—sparked by Rosa Parks' refusal to give up her seat to a white passenger—was later seen as Act One of the Civil Rights Movement. For perhaps the first time, a horrified nation saw firsthand how segregation laws were used against innocent African Americans. As a result of the Parks' incident, King launched a public relations campaign to eliminate these laws in the South. He also confirmed that a peaceful response could overcome ignorance and violence.

The campaign lasted until 1956, when the U.S. Supreme Court ruled in *Browder v. Gayle* that the segregation law in Alabama was unconstitutional. The successful litigation of Montgomery citizens, heavily backed by the National Association of the Advancement of Colored People (NAACP) set the trajectory for King's subsequent leadership of the Civil Rights Movement.

The Birmingham, Alabama, Protest, 1963

The nonviolent Birmingham protest in 1963 was King's first attempt at applying his public relations strategy against a political adversary. King gathered African American men and women to protest injustices within the city's police department, particularly targeting the commissioner Eugene "Bull" Conner—a known racist (Greenbaum 2013, p. 2). King's campaign was called Project C, for "Confrontation," and it included press conferences, leaflets, and demonstrations in front of the media (Hanson 2012). On April 3rd, activists began staging sit-ins in local restaurants, refusing to sit in advertised "Blacks" segregated areas (Greenbaum 2013, p. 2). These actions led to a strong response from the Birmingham police force as King had envisaged when he developed his strategy. Network TV, radio, and national newspapers like *The New York Times* and *Washington Post* captured images portraying the gravity of the Birmingham situation. For the first time, thanks to the press coverage, Americans nationwide were beginning to see how the black population was still being treated in the South.

There was another phase to King's plan in Birmingham: not only did he use the media to expose conditions for Southern blacks; he also decided to involve third parties, a well-established public relations technique to add credibility to messages. Thus, he encouraged high-profile men to personally experience what segregation laws actually felt like. On April 12th, King was joined in Birmingham by Ralph Abernathy, King's right-hand man and most trusted friend, to march in the street in protest, despite an injunction ruled on two days earlier (Greene 2014). On April 26th, however, King, Abernathy, and 11 other African Americans involved in the march were sentenced to five days in a Birmingham jail (Greenbaum 2013, p. 2).

It was inside the jail walls that King wrote the famous "Letter from Birmingham Jail." Although King directed the letter to eight white religious leaders in the South, he also used it as a tool to deliver messages to the public. King ("The Negro is Your Brother" 1963, pp. 78–88) wrote, "Injustice anywhere is a threat to justice everywhere. We are caught in an inescapable network of mutuality, tied in a single garment of destiny. Whatever affects one directly affects all indirectly. Never again can we afford to live with the narrow, provincial 'outside agitator' idea."

King aimed to remind the leaders—as well as the public and political establishment—that *all* Americans are affected by the injustice upon the African Americans. King drew on scripture teachings of morality to emphasize the injustice: "All segregation statutes are unjust because segregation distorts the soul and damages the personality. It gives the segregator a false sense of superiority and the segregated a false sense of inferiority" (King 1963, n.d., pp. 78–88). Finally, in describing the purpose of the movement, King wrote that it is "nourished by the contemporary frustration over the continued existence of racial discrimination. It is made up of people who have lost faith in America. . ."

Yet, perhaps the greatest and most profound act of the Birmingham protest came next, proving to impact hearts and minds throughout the country. It occurred on May 2nd with the "Children Marches," during which police arrested nearly a thousand children. Birmingham jails were overwhelmed. City officials took to even more brutal tactics: they ordered firefighters to spray the children with water hoses and demanded police use clubs and dogs to frighten the child-protestors. "Television brought the dramatic visuals into the living rooms all across America." (Greenbaum 2013, p. 2)

On May 10, officials and civil rights leaders came to a settlement. Officials agreed that African Americans could be allowed back into public spaces, transportation, and jobs. They also released the activists from jail. Television cameras brought the barbaric scenes of police brutality into the nation's living rooms evening after evening. Radio and print journalists, reporting from the streets of Birmingham, gave dramatic first-person coverage of events that were once unimaginable in the United States. Despite the widespread media, however, King realized that in order to achieve social justice for African Americans throughout the country, he needed to start appearing outside of the South.

The March on Washington, 1963

The next public took place August 28. The historic March on Washington drew crowds of nearly 300,000 and televised by all three networks ("Letter from the Birmingham Jail," 1963). King, now 34, could not pass up a demonstration of this magnitude. Originally devised in 1941 by A. Philip Randolph, president of the Sleeping Car Porters of America, the massive demonstration required detailed planning (Elliott 1991, p. 10). Randolph partnered with Bayard Rustin, an openly gay organizer and strategist, who organized the logistics of the campaign. Volunteers prepared 80,000 50-cent boxed lunches (consisting of a cheese sandwich, a slice of pound cake, and an apple) (Fletcher and Reed 2013). According to an article run years later in *Newsweek* (September 2, 1963):

> In Washington, 26 public toilets were set up, each with facilities for up to 40 persons. There were 22 first-aid stations, staffed with two doctors and four nurses apiece. And thousands of District of Columbia police, National Guardsmen and volunteer marshals stood by to maintain order, if needed (they weren't). More than 1,500 chartered buses rumbled into Washington, and on the morning of the march 40 special trains pulled into Union Station at the rate of one every few minutes.

King, along with several other civil rights activists, rallied at the monument once built to commemorate President Lincoln's efforts to abolish slavery and the ratification of the 13th Amendment.

The quality of speechwriting for King, as well as the other civil rights speakers of the day, was of critical importance. According to Fletcher and Reed (2013), John Lewis recalled, "We tried to come up with a speech that would represent the young people: the foot soldiers, people on the front lines." He said, "If we do not see meaningful progress here today, we will march through cities, towns and hamlets and villages all across America" (Fletcher and Reed 2013). To the thousands on site, and to the millions listening on radio and television, King delivered one of the most consequential and memorable speeches of all time. Julian Bond recollected later in an oral history, "His speech began with a slow, slow cadence at first and then picked up speed and going faster and faster. You saw what a magnificent speechmaker he was, and you knew something important was happening" (Fletcher and Reed 2013).

In this, his famous "I Have a Dream" speech, King stressed the need to end police brutality and the need to maintain vigilance in response to injustice. While reciting lines "My Country 'Tis of Thee," he concluded his speech with powerful spiritual overtones, ". . . All of God's children, black men and white men, Jews and Gentiles, Protestants and Catholics will be able to join hands and sing the words of the old Negro spiritual, free at last, free at last, thank God almighty we're free at last!" (Hanson 2012).

According to the *Smithsonian* magazine (2013), the March on Washington was the climax of the Civil Rights Movement. Fletcher and Reed (2013) noted from multiple sources the impact this speech made. For instance, Ken Howard, a DC student intern working in Washington at the time recalled, "There was an expectation and excitement that this march finally would make a difference." Howard continued, "The March on Washington symbolized a rising up, if you will, of people who were saying enough is enough." Rachelle Horowitz, aide to civil rights leader Bayard Rustin, recollected, "Originally it was conceived of as a march for jobs, but as 1963 progressed, with the Birmingham demonstrations, the assassination of Medgar Evers and the introduction of the Civil Rights Act by President Kennedy, it became clear that it had to be a march for jobs *and* for freedom."

John Lewis, Chairman of the Student Non-Violent Coordinating Committee (SNCC) and 13-term Congressman from Georgia, arranged a preliminary meeting for King with President Kennedy, remarking, "It was the so-called 'Big Six,' Randolph, James Farmer, Whitney Young, Roy Wilkins, Martin Luther King, Jr. and myself" (Fletcher and Reed 2013). Lewis recalled that before the March, President Kennedy was concerned about the "violence and chaos and disorder" that might occur in the Capitol. But as soon King commenced his speech President Kennedy's concerns were laid to rest. Advocating for "meeting physical force with *soul* force," King, repeatedly called on Americans to protest peacefully. The March proved to have the impact on the nation's civil rights debate that King was hoping for: the public and politicians started paying closer attention to the racial injustices of the South.

Another reason for the March's success was King's use of celebrities. Harry Belafonte told the *Smithsonian Magazine* (2013), "Dr. King saw that as hugely strategic." As Belafonte recollected, "My job was to convince the icons in the arts that they needed to have a presence in Washington on that day." The power of the six men standing behind him meant a great deal to King, but he also encouraged the "Big Six" to stand among the people. Belafonte said, "We had to seize this opportunity and make our voices heard. Make those who are comfortable with our oppression uncomfortable." Andrew Young, aide to King at the SCLC said, "the plan was to include not only SCLC but all of the civil rights organizations . . . we had a big contingent from Hollywood." Belafonte had also asked the white actor Marlon Brando to chair the leading delegation from California (Fletcher and Reed 2013). In fact, this tactic was so successful it was copied on the 50th Anniversary celebration of the March with celebrities like Oprah and Jamie Foxx (Bihm 2013).

King said that the March on Washington was the greatest demonstration in the history of our nation. He expressed his view that it not only raised awareness for the Civil Rights Movement, but also that it inspired thousands of Northerners to journey South to protest peacefully for equality.

The Selma to Montgomery March, 1965

The next event in King's campaign was the Selma to Montgomery, Alabama, march in 1965. Civil rights leaders, including Dr. King, made the march to press for voting rights in the state. Like the March on Washington, the Selma to Montgomery event was planned to be a peaceful protest. What was not planned was the blockade put up by more than 150 police officials at the end of the Edmund Pettus Bridge. The blockade, and the events that occurred thereafter, made Selma a strategically important event showcasing police brutality and injustice.

The Selma to Montgomery March began in prayer on the grounds of a local church. Led by Hosea Williams and John Lewis of the SNCC, some 600 men and women of all races assembled in Selma. Similar to the March on Washington, King as well as his close friend John Lewis linked arms and led the procession. In a transcript of John Lewis' testimony on March 7th he states, "We were able to move about 50 feet, and at that time a state trooper made an announcement on a bullhorn or megaphone, and he said, 'This march will not continue.'" According to Lewis' later testimony, a state trooper announced, "this is an unlawful assembly. This demonstration will not continue. You have been banned by the governor. I am going to order you to disperse." Lewis testified that police officials took up positions and began moving into the crowd "knocking us down and pushing us." What began as a peaceful march between two cities soon came to be called "Bloody Sunday."

Shocking images of police brutality appeared, once again, on television news and the front pages of dailies nationwide. Somehow, all the ground King and his fellow civil rights leaders made in Washington did not seem to have reached the South. For King, peaceful protest was a constitutional right and, therefore, he reasoned, the police blockade in Selma was against the law. King quickly adjusted his strategy so that it became more about the illegal blockade and police brutality, rather than a peaceful march for voting rights.

In an article for *The Miami Times* (2014), Joseph A. Califano, Jr., President Lyndon B. Johnson's former top aide on Domestic Affairs, asserted that the principal architect behind Selma was President Johnson, not King (Guniss 2014). "In fact, Selma was LBJ's idea. He considered the Voting Rights Act his greatest legislative achievement, and he viewed King as an essential partner in getting it enacted . . ." (pp. 1C, 6C). But Califano's assertion was called into question by Paul Webb's script for the film, "Selma," (IMDB, "Selma" Paul Webb, 2014) which portrays Johnson instead as a reluctant champion of the Act. The film shows how King used the march to pressure the President to move ahead with the bill's passage.

In a transcription written by King ("Equality Now" 1961) regarding his approach in 1964 he wrote, "Federal power is enormous and amply sufficient to guide us through the changes ahead" ("Equality Now" 1954–1968). King goes on, "If we would search for the key problem in the intolerably slow progress in civil rights, we will find that the self-imposed limits in the case of bold, creative Federal action constitute barriers as difficult as those erected by the opposition." King saw the Selma march as a way to break down those barriers and push the Federal government to action.

Fifty years later, Selma is seen as a key turning point in the Civil Rights Movement, primarily because of the unprecedented violence caused by local officials. Part of King's strategy was to expose to the world a justice system that had long been preventing peaceful protests from taking place in the South. The Selma to Montgomery March paved the way for uninhibited peaceful protests in America. Events in Selma also provided a glimpse into the personal distrust King held for the workings of government, especially when it prevented nationwide progress in the protection of civil rights.

King's Influence

On April 4, 1968, Dr. Martin Luther King was assassinated in Memphis, Tennessee. He was 39 years old. *The Seattle Times* (2011) summarized King's achievements, saying in an editorial "At 33, he was pressing the case of civil rights with President John Kennedy. At 34, he galvanized the nation with his 'I Have a Dream' speech. At 35, he won the Nobel Peace Prize. At 39, he was assassinated, but he left a legacy of hope and inspiration that continues today." King's influence was a shining beacon on injustice and inequality, a fight that continues today. These three major events present King's unparalleled ability to influence the public and the government during the American Civil Rights Movement of the 1950s and 1960s using the strategies, tools, and tactics of classic public relations practice.

He brought the issue to life by galvanizing thousands of people at massive public events, as well as those who watched and listened to the events at home. He involved third party endorsers—celebrities and government officials, as well as other civil right leaders—to add credibility and objectivity to his message. He used strategic media coverage to bring his messages of discrimination, violence, and police brutality to the world. And he inspired Americans—north and south alike—through the use of soulful rhetoric, religious in spirit, to give voice to his unwavering pursuit of justice, peace, and equality.

Conclusion

These three events changed the tone, as well as the model for future civil rights campaigns in America. Dr. King's efforts demonstrate the effectiveness of thoughtful, well-planned public relations efforts in support of an issue. His model set the stage for progress across a wide array of civil rights issues—from the women's movement to gay rights, as well as to the right to universal vote, finally given to African Americans in Voting Rights Act, two years after King's assassination.

Takeaway

The use of strategic public relations to influence attitudes and build support for favorable public policies live on as a critical part of Dr. King's legacy. For him, the highly sensitive and complex process of developing a successful civil rights campaign was dependent on drawing huge numbers of people to the cause. His enormous appeal—which seemed to grow with every appearance—produced great volumes of front-page coverage and precious access to government leaders. His strategy was simply to participate, lead by example, and communicate authentically.

As with Betty Freidan, King's message came at just the right time. The rebellious mood of the country—with "equal rights" being at the forefront of the fervor—enabled King's rhetoric to light a match under an already fueled-up society.

Public relations professionals today can learn a lot from his example of actions and words that drove a profound change in America.

CHAPTER 11

The Triangle Shirtwaist Factory Fire and the Rise of the Labor Safety Movement

Historians have called the 1911 Triangle Shirtwaist Factory fire a catalyst in the American labor movement. The tragic event—a result of a locked emergency exit—ignited strikes, outrage, and the mobilization of a major grassroots labor safety movement whose influence is still felt today. Although the Triangle fire occurred more than a century ago, research conducted by historians proves the event was one of the most transformative developments in American social and economic history, forever changing the "traditional war between capital and labor" and the responsibilities the federal government in protecting its workers.

Placing responsibility with the government for labor safety was contrary to the beliefs common in the "Gilded Age," but central to the worker-rights philosophies of the upcoming Progressive Era.

Background

On March 25, 1911, New Yorkers witnessed the deadliest industrial accident in the history of the country. The Triangle Shirtwaist Company, one of the city's largest factories, specialized in the manufacturing of dresses, more specifically, the highly fashionable shirtwaist dress so popular at the time. The company and its owners were very well-known in fashion circles and the city's business elite.

Occupying the top three floors of the Asch Building, a 10-story skyscraper at the corner of Washington Place and Greene Street in Lower Manhattan, the Triangle Company went up in flames one Saturday afternoon and left 146 workers dead (Charles 2006). The September 11, 2001, terrorist attacks on the World Trade Center, is the only workplace fire in history that took more lives (Marrin 2011). Investigators would prove that the Triangle fire was caused by indifference toward the well-being of its young workers and an absence of adequate safety measures—such as emergency exits, alarm systems, and fire escapes.

Historian Albert Marrin compared workplace safety standards during the 19th century to the labor laws enforced today. In his book, titled, *Flesh & Blood So Cheap: The Triangle Fire and Its Legacy,* Marrin (2011) explains, "There was no health insurance or Medicare . . . no old age pensions or Social Security . . . no unemployment benefits . . . no laws regulating hours and wages and zero safety and sanitation standards." If you were hurt or killed at work, that was just too bad.

The Triangle factory was typical for the era, and in some ways, even better than some. As with most factories of the time, it employed cheap labor—young immigrant girls whose paychecks went directly to pay their families' rent and food. With jobs scarce and workers plentiful, factory owners had little incentive to improve working conditions. Besides, any improvements would cost money, taking a bite out of profit margins (already squeezed, in the case of Triangle, by a decline in popularity for the shirtwaist). The accepted wisdom of the Industrial Age was that workers were dispensable objects, just around to produce profit, no more valuable than their spools of threads and darning needles. In fact, many would even claim that a sewing machine was quite a bit more valuable than the girl who operated it.

But events of the Triangle fire caused a major attitude shift. Encouraged by a carefully orchestrated public relations campaign, the public demanded that the government step in to enact worker safety laws. These mandates not only protected employees, they encouraged mutually beneficial relationships between management and workers, government and company, and company with its customers and local communities. Companies eventually saw the value of working in the public interest—an early foray into corporate social responsibility philosophies of today.

Poverty and Immigration

By the turn of the century, three out of four people lived in poverty (Marrin 2011). To make matters worse, workplace conditions were unhealthy and dangerous. In 1911, more than 50,000 people died while on the job—that is, about 1,000 each week, or 140 a day, every day. Despite these high numbers, people continued to land on the shores of Manhattan, the Land of Opportunity. Families from southern and eastern Europe—Italy, Greece, Hungary, Romania, Poland, and Russia—made up seven out of ten immigrants entering the United States (Burns and Sanders, *New York: An Illustrated History* 1999). The vast majority were impoverished Italians and Russian Jews, who came to America carrying only what they could hold on their backs. They needed to work, no matter the conditions, no matter the pay.

The Triangle fire came during the greatest mass exodus of Europeans ever to occur. By the early 1900s, America had become a nation of fast-growing, prosperous cities, making it widely attractive to those facing political and religious persecution in Europe. For Italians, after surviving the Messina earthquake and tsunami, the United States seemed like a Mecca (Odencrantz 1919). Southern Italians, particularly in Sicily, had long felt contempt from their northern countrymen, who frequently referred to them as "Black Italians" or "Africans" as a way to diminish their significance in a racist way (Russell-Ciardi n.d.).

Russian Jews faced mounting religious persecution under the Tsarist regime. Russians called them "Christ killers" and used Jews as scapegoats during bad economic times. A popular strategy the Russians used to further oppress Jews was called pogroms—meaning "riot" or "devastation" in Russian (Dworkin 2000). In April 1903, Spitzer (2013) cited a *New York Times* article described a typical pogrom, saying, ". . .Babes were literally torn to pieces by the frenzied and bloodthirsty mob. The local police made no attempt to check the reign of terror. In just 3 years, some 3,100 Russian Jews died from pogroms" (Spitzer 2013). Forced to live under such relentlessly harsh conditions, thousands of Russian Jews found refuge in America.

New York City: Don't Believe the Hype

Typical immigrants had never been outside their own small towns, much less ever seen New York firsthand. New York had an image in Europe as an ultra-modern paradise, its people flaunting all the new conveniences of the modern age—telephones, electric lights, and even motorcars. Society ladies were portrayed in Europe wearing high hats, bustling across Fifth

Avenue guided by their husbands, wealthy industrialists, and riding in bejeweled carriages to their mansions uptown.

This was the New York the immigrants pictured. But it was not the New York that awaited them. After disembarking from the 7-day voyage in steerage, a horrifying scene awaited them. The streets, rather than being paved with gold, were covered in garbage (Marrin 2011).

Despite this grim reality, the newcomers appreciated their new home. Here they could make a living, practice their religion freely, and even raise a family. For the first time they had access to free public school education, where many learned to read and write English. They marveled at the department stores, streetlamps, and even a new type of train that ran underground, the "subway" (Hood 2004). With more and more companies starting up in lower Manhattan, officials wondered how to squeeze even more people, more buildings, and more factories into such a limited area. It did not take long before architects began sorting those issues out, and by 1913 Manhattan had what was then the tallest building on earth, the 55-story Woolworth Building (Weiss 1992).

Immigrant Living Conditions and Workplace Hazards

According to Marrin (2011), to meet the rising demand for immigrant housing in the 1880s, landlords built "dumbbell tenement" apartment buildings up to six stories high, designed to house as many families as could possibly fit. The crowding caused unhealthy, uncomfortable, and unsafe living conditions—hardly the life the immigrants imagined back in Europe. In 1890, photojournalist Jacob Riis (Yochelson and Czitrom 2014) made history by going into the tenements and photographing immigrant families, using the newly invented flash powder. It was the first time immigrant life was documented for the rest of the world to see.

The immigrants faced unsafe working conditions as well. "One newspaper reporter [told of] a group of Italian immigrants laying subway track: 'The men were torn and mangled and their blood was scattered all over the tracks'" (Marrin 2011).

Such tragedies, whether in the building trades or factories, happened with increasing frequency, a function of a metropolis now burgeoning at breakneck speed.

Innovation and Symbols of Women's Liberation

New manufacturing technologies allowed for mass production of clothing, which meant for the first time customers could buy ready-made clothes right off the shelves. Ordinary people could now afford to buy the latest new fashions from Paris, no longer needing to depend on tailors or mothers making clothes one garment at a time.

According the Nancy L. Green (1997), ready-to-wear clothing also now came in standard sizes, for everything from winter coats to undergarments. This enabled people to use clothing to express their individual personalities and status. Newspaper ads showcased "well-made, elegant clothing" that consumers could wear as a symbol of social rank (Marrin 2011). Manufacturing for blouses alone doubled within a decade, and New York became known as the capital of ready-made clothing (von Drehle 2004). The shirtwaist was the most sought after style of them all.

The "Shirtwaist Kings"

Max Blanck and Isaac Harris, also known as the "Shirtwaist Kings," were the leading manufacturers of shirtwaists. The workers used descriptors for the two bosses that harkened back to the political strife they faced in Europe. They secretly called them "dictators" and "czars" (Linder 2007). The workers' complaints were rooted in long hours, poor working conditions, and low pay. They were required to work 9-hour days (seven on Saturdays). They were crammed into tiny workspaces and were charged for the thread, needles, and fabric they used. For the 52-hour workweek they earned between $7 and $12.

Blanck and Harris made sure to keep the doors locked. This, they thought, would prevent workers from taking breaks or stealing pieces of fabric (https://www.natcom.org/CommCurrentsArticle.aspx?id=1967). And, as Marrin (2011) notes, because they feared losing their jobs, workers could never challenge management about any of the policies, even the noticeable lack of safety procedures. They could be fired for any reason or no reason at all, and the workers could do nothing about it.

The Rise of the Labor Movement

Only by joining trade unions could workers use their combined power to balance the owners' power. Trade unions work to improve the wages, hours, and working conditions of its members, mainly through a type of negotiating known as collective bargaining (Katz, Kuruvilla and, Turner 1993). When collective bargaining fails, unions go on strikes, attracting widespread attention from the public and the press.

In September 1909, three years before the fire, some of the Triangle factory workers went on strike in a walkout that was one of the first labor actions in the garment industry. Their action prompted other workers in the industry to go on strike to bring public attention to their intolerable working conditions. The movement became known as the "Uprising of 20,000," because 20,000 of the nation's 32,000 shirtwaist workers went on strike.

The workers called for union representation, something that the owners were vehemently against. To counter their efforts and demonstrate the power they still held over the workers, Blanck and Harris devised a plan of what today would be called "dirty tricks." They hired local prostitutes and ex-prize fighters to pick fights with the women on the picket lines. They convinced violent gangsters to cause injury or even kill the picketers, and paid them only few dollars (Linder 2007). They bribed the police to arrest workers who fought back and bribed judges who eventually found the workers guilty.

The strike was recognized as the largest by women ever seen in the United States. The women's demands included "An end to the subcontracting system, a 52-hour work week with unpaid overtime limited to two hours per day, and an end to wage deductions for supplies and electricity" (Pool 2012). On one side, some saw the uprising as more than a struggle over wages and working conditions. On the other side, people who called themselves "feminists," genuinely believed in the equality of political and social rights for women. The strikers' slogan was, "We'd rather starve quick than starve slow" (Drainville 2013). This is when the media and public started becoming increasingly sympathetic to the strikers.

Alva Belmont, the rich widow of a millionaire banker and daughter of a railway tycoon, helped create the "Mink Coat Brigade," a group of wealthy women who went out to aid the strikers (Marrin 2011). Because of their fame and wealth, the Mink Coat Brigade managed to keep the strikers in the press on a daily basis. The wealthy ladies standing next to the immigrant picketers made for irresistible photos, stories, and newsreels. The women also arranged for human interest stories to be told by the young workers—in their Italian and Yiddish accents—before crowds of reporters and cameramen. The Brigade knew that those personal testimonials, presented in broken English with native accents, would enhance the emotional appeal greatly (Marrin 2011). The strategy worked. Subsequently, influential business titans like Andrew Carnegie provided funds to keep the movement going.

Blanck negotiated secretly with union leaders and reached agreement on the strikers' demands. According to Marrin (2011), "They agreed on a 12 percent pay raise, a 52-hour work week, and an end to petty abuses like charging for needles and chairs."

Reactions to the Fire

On March 11, 1911, as the workers at the Triangle Building were finishing up their day, a fire of uncertain origin started to flare up underneath a huge pile of cloth scraps. As smoke permeated throughout the 8th, 9th, and 10th floors, panicked workers tore through the aisles looking for emergency exits, open stairways, fire escapes, or even a way up to the roof. The luckiest ones managed to jam into the elevator or find their way to the roof. But with the emergency doors to the street locked (as a measure to against workers trying to steal) workers were forced to try other routes out. Many sought safety on a flimsy staircase, but it collapsed under the weight of the workers, spilling dozens 100 feet to their deaths on the concrete sidewalks. Others tried to escape by jumping onto the elevator shaft, but once the elevator collapsed, these workers, too, ended up plunging to their deaths. Still dozens had no choice but to flee out of the windows and onto the street, eight stories below. In all, 146 workers died: 123 women and 23 men, the majority between the ages of 16 and 23, all recent immigrants.

The fire became a major turning point in the efforts to create safer working conditions throughout the United States. Until then, the city had no laws requiring sprinklers or fire drills (McEvoy 1995). Years later, it became painfully obvious that a single ceiling sprinkler might have saved the lives of every factory worker at the Triangle factory that day.

And, fire drills could have served to reduce the rampant panic, which contributed to many of the deaths.

News coverage of the event was especially effective at paving the way for new laws to emerge (Jensen, Doss, and Ivic 2011). In 1911, the only media channels available were newspapers and the telegraph wire services that fed stories to them. Without being able to see the pictures themselves, the public had to rely totally on journalists' descriptions of major events and other newsworthy topics.

Highly descriptive and detailed coverage ran in *The New York Times*, for instance. Reporters interviewed the survivors to get their firsthand accounts of the workers' attempts to escape—the crowds overcome by flames and asphyxiated by smoke. From all accounts, it appeared that the victims of this industrial deathtrap never had the slightest chance of escaping the blazing building.

Effectiveness of Efforts

Immediately, in response to the tragedy, New Yorkers gave generous donations to victims and their families. Furthermore, the American Red Cross, the WTUL, the ILGWU, and many civic organizations took up collections (Marrin 2011). The reforms that followed the Triangle fire became models for federal labor policies. By the time of the fire, 85 percent of all shirtwaist makers in New York had belonged to the ILGWU (Bao 2001).

Blanck and Harris were arrested and charged with six counts of manslaughter in the death of two of the 146 workers who died in the fire. Marrin (2011) reports the creation of The New York Factory Investigating Commission, serving a total of four years, investigating 3,385 workplaces, questioning 472 witnesses, and taking over 7,000 pages of testimony. Its findings advanced a new idea about the role of government in protecting American life. Information collected by the commission led to a total of thirty-four laws, which influence labor safety laws to this day.

Conclusion

Overcrowded factories with poor ventilation and inadequate toilet facilities are still a reality to many workers around the world, especially those living in underdeveloped countries. For example, the world's poorest country, Bangladesh, has seen its share of workplace disasters, including several deadly fires culminating from a lack of fire safety rules or guidelines. In 2013, it suffered one of the deadliest garment factory accidents in its history (http://observer.com/2015/05/horrifying-documentary-will-change-the-way-you-think-about-shopping/ 2015), capturing the attention of the public worldwide. The Rana Plaza garment factory in Dhaka, Bangladesh, collapsed, killing over a thousand people and wounding thousands more. Rallies and pressure from Bangladesh's overseas trading partners, particularly the United States, persuaded the government to order safety improvements. However, these still have a long way to go.

In order to prevent history from repeating itself, today's private groups—like the National Labor Committee, United Students Against Sweatshops, International Labor Rights Fund, and other organizations are working to raise American awareness about sweatshops, especially those located overseas.

Takeaway

Crisis often breeds change. It rouses a once-indifferent population to pay heed to the plight of its victims—and seek justice for the perpetrators.

The fires at the "Triangle Shirtwaist Factory" exposed a world few had ever before seen. Now featured in gruesome detail on Page One of nearly every daily paper, the tragedy unearthed a hidden but widespread American plague: the insidious working conditions of newly arrived immigrants and the government policies, and lack thereof, that caused them. Shameful was a country that one day opens its arms to welcome the "weary and poor" and the next, allows them to die.

In this case, grassroots, advocacy campaigns—organizing marches, rallies, and protests—brought media attention to the abuses workers experienced in garment factories. It led to new legislation mandating improved working conditions for laborers, and held factory owners accountable for maintaining the standards. Decades later, a federal body was created specifically to enforce the new laws—the Occupational Safety Hazards Agency.

While working conditions in America and the protection of workers has improved dramatically, the rest of the world—particularly in developing countries—needs to catch up. Public relations—either conducted by grassroots organizations or by professionals—will surely play a role in making that happen.

CHAPTER 12

The Fight against Income Inequality

From Huey Long to Occupy Wall Street

Many popular expressions about income inequality from the past century (e.g., "We are the 99%," "Share the wealth," "A chicken in every pot") have enjoyed the public limelight at some point or another. And while each may reflect a different political, economic, and social climate, they all represent a battle cry heard far and wide through the decades.

The income inequality movement—emerging in the Progressive era of the early 1900s and reappearing in 2011—has campaigned to ask society to look under the glossy sheen of the "world's wealthiest country" and instead see an economy that appears to be stacked against the vast majority of citizens. The movement points to the continually growing gap between the "haves" and the "have-nots" as the cause all too many to give up on the American dream.

Income inequality is not new in America. But the earliest statistics we are able to find are from the early part of the 20th century. At that time—the era of the Rockefellers, Vanderbilts, and Carnegies—the richest 1 percent of Americans controlled roughly 18 percent of all income.

Some 70 years later that gap had grown by 6 percent, which represents a disparity of tens of billions of dollars. By 2007, the top one percent accounted for 24 percent (Slote 2010).

The Beginnings of a Movement

The first campaigns railing against income inequality were triggered by the Great Depression, which began in America in 1929. Lasting 10 years, it was the deepest and longest-lasting economic downturn in the history of the Western industrialized world ("The Great Depression" n.d.). The stock market crashed, consumer spending declined, and unemployment reached unprecedented proportions. By 1933, when the Great Depression reached its nadir, some 13 to 15 million Americans were unemployed and nearly half of the country's banks had failed.

From the darkness of the Depression came two notable campaigns that brought this issue to the forefront of the national attention. Senator Huey Long's 1932 Senatorial campaign championed the idea that every man should be a king (Amenta, Kathleen, and Mary 1994). And socialist writer Upton Sinclair ran for Governor of California on a redistribution of wealth platform called EPIC ("Upton Sinclair, the California EPIC Movement–1934" 2015). And later came the 2011 #OccupyWallStreet campaign.

These programs are milestone movements because of the communications campaigns that drove them. The news coverage not only brought "income inequality" to the forefront, it gave voice to a once "silent majority." It also managed to put in easy-to-understand terms what this disparity was all about, and what the long-term consequences would be if these trends continued. Finally, the smart messaging—like, "we are the 99 percent"—brought the message home to the American public, and also helped fuel the anti-Romney sentiment of the 2012 U.S. presidential election.

Huey Long

In the early years of the Great Depression, Huey Long, the one-time governor of Louisiana, campaigned for a U.S. Senate seat, leveraging the timely issue of income inequality and bringing it for the first time to the forefront of the national agenda. Doing this demonstrated his compassion for the common man—who most likely was out of work and securing meager rations on bread lines. With the phrase, "Every man a king!" he showed Americans that he believed in them, that they, too, deserved better in this life. Finally, there was someone in Washington who "felt" their pain and knew how to fix it. Masterfully seizing upon the newest technology of the day—talking pictures—he managed to build a more intimate and trusting relationship with the public than many other politicians of the day. He continued using "income disparity" as this platform long after his successful bid for the Senate to pave the way for his presidential campaign in 1936 (Amenta n.d.).

Senator Long frequently spoke of this disparity by framing it in statistics: 85 percent of the wealth in the nation was owned by 4 percent of the people. In his speeches, he often used the analogy of diners at a barbeque, asking, "What should be done when one man comes in to a barbeque and takes what is meant for 9/10 of the people to eat?" His answer was "make that man come back and give back some of the grub he ain't got no business with" (Amenta n.d.). Most often, the line was met by thunderous applause and showers of laughter from the crowds.

At the time, Long's views were seen by many as extreme. And charges of corruption swirled around him, eroding the trust and credibility he had built. The Louisiana State Legislature tried, but failed to impeach him. His many detractors fought against his popularity through negative comments in the press and through the popular new communications tool of newsreels—film compilations of news stories presented in movie theatres in the first half of the century. In a newsreel, the voice-over rather bluntly declares that under Long's leadership, the State of Louisiana "is in the grip of a decidedly un-American dictator" ("Radio's America: The Great Depression and the Rise of Modern Mass Culture" 2015).

But Long remained steadfast in his views about what was needed to help the American economy, and continued to campaign for an improvement in the nation's income distribution. He even founded "Share Our Wealth" clubs in communities across the country. By 1935, the height of the Depression, active membership was 7.5 million. On his radio interviews, he regularly drew more than 25 million listeners. And for years, more than 60,000 supporters sent him letters (more than President Roosevelt was receiving) (Amenta n.d.).

Upton Sinclair

Upton Sinclair, one of the most prolific writers of the Progressive Era, is perhaps best known for his "muckraking" activities. Muckrakers were investigative journalists who "dug up the dirt" on unscrupulous business and political practices and used the press to expose the many social ills of our increasingly industrialized, over-populated cities. Sinclair's first book, and perhaps the one that most readers associate with him, is *The Jungle*, a brutal expose of the unsanitary conditions of meatpacking factories. Published in 1906, the book sparked a public uproar. The fallout led to the creation of the Pure Food and Drug and the Meat Inspection Acts ("Tour the Project" 2015).

In 1934, after publishing several successful books, Sinclair set out for politics, running for governor in hope of improving conditions for the people of California. Much like Huey Long, Sinclair tied his political campaign to the income inequality issue, which resonated well with Depression-era audiences. While vast numbers of people throughout the country were going hungry, California farmers were literally burning their crops due to overproduction.

Thus, Sinclair created a plan called End Poverty In California (EPIC). He proposed that available land in California be used for cooperatives where inhabitants would live peacefully and share labor and crops with each other ("Tour the Project" n.d.). But to many in politics, the EPIC plan, as much as it would help starving citizens, reeked of socialism. And for that reason, opponents railed against it, and him, in the media.

One high-profile part of the campaign against Sinclair was a faked newsreel item. It seemed to show every day Americans "spontaneously" sharing their views, connecting the EPIC plan with the Russian government, and claiming the programs seemed radical. While on the surface the film seemed real, it was ultimately proven by *Variety* magazine to be a fake, produced by Hollywood movie mogul Louis B. Mayer. This is considered by many to be the earliest use of "attack" advertising in America ("The Campaign of the Century," Mitchell, Random House 1992).

The Financial Crisis of 2008

The most recent cries for "income inequality" were borne of the "Great Recession," following the "Financial Crisis" of 2008. The damage it caused to economies around the world, as well as on the lives of the vast majority of Americans, was second only to that caused by the Great Depression.

The major cause cited for the 2008 crash was the rampant issuance of "sub-prime mortgages"—cheap home loans given out to people with poor credit—during a time in the early 2000s when home values across the United States were skyrocketing. Everyone, especially first-time homebuyers, wanted "in" on the action. And the banks were only too happy to encourage them—advertising "no interest, no money down" mortgages. Unlike the "old" days when banks would be responsible for collecting the monthly mortgages, banks now were able to get the loans off their books immediately after they were granted. So there was little risk involved. Once the banks made the loans, they instantly sold them off to the big investment banks on Wall Street, who then repackaged them into complex financial products, and marketed as investments to unsuspecting buyers. What the investors did not know was that these portfolios of home loans—"mortgage-backed securities"—would one day turn into "toxic assets" and practically overnight poison every aspect of the economy.

After the height of the real estate market, prices for these homes began to drop precipitously. Interest rates rose on the mortgages, far more than what the new homeowners were able to pay. Many soon found themselves "underwater," owing more debt than the value of their homes.

What started so innocently on Main Street was now threatening the very survival of Wall Street. Banks that had so heavily invested in these bad home loans now found themselves scurrying to cover their losses, causing the credit markets to all but seize. Under the weight of plummeting stock prices, failing finances and loss of public confidence, two of Wall Street's legends—Bear Stearns and Lehman Brothers—failed within months of each other. Others were soon to follow, had it not been for the intervention of the Federal Reserve in September 2008, and the enactment of the Troubled Assets Relief Program. The government's intervention prevented an all-out economic apocalypse, far greater than even the Great Depression. But, while the banks were saved, the rages of economic destruction swept across the nation—stealing jobs, homes, security, and dreams, leaving very little in its path unscathed.

Occupy Wall Street

The Financial Crisis was felt by all but a small, and very lucky, percentage of the public. Thus, it was no surprise that income disparity became greater anytime in history. From 2008–2010, while the vast majority of households suffered enormous financial losses, the top 1 percent increased their share of wealth by nearly 40 percent (Wolf 2010).

This created a new opportunity to speak out against the disparity between the rich and the poor. The Internet, smart phones, and social media all helped to create a landscape, at the turn of the 21st century, that was very different from what had existed for Senator Huey Long and Upton Sinclair. People gained the ability to connect instantly with one another through the Internet, even if they lived in different parts of the country or the world. A single individual was empowered by having easy access to a video camera, which came as part of the increasingly ubiquitous "smart phone." Facebook, Twitter, and Instagram gave people the ability to post videos on the Internet instantly and to reach potential viewers all around the world.

The Occupy Wall Street movement burst onto the scene during this age of social media when its protesters filled the streets of Manhattan on September 17, 2011 ("A Message From Occupied Wall Street Day Five," Web. 29 May 2015).

Occupy was inspired by social movements in Egypt and Tunisia during the same year that the movement launched. While it was known as a leaderless movement, Kalle Lasn is known for originating the call to action, and Micah White assisted him. Social media played a major role in helping Occupy organize itself into a movement. In early June of 2011 the domain name OccupyWallStreet.org was registered by Lasn, and 90,000 of the Subscribers of Adbusters (the media organization he ran) were emailed with the subject line: "America Needs Its Own Tahrir" ("Pre-Occupied" 2015).

The email referred to the name of the park, literally translated as "Liberation Square," in Cairo where the "Arab Spring" protests began.

In New York, protesters gathered in September 2011 in Zuccotti Park, located in the city's financial district. They adopted the slogan "we are the 99%" and took their messages about income inequality to the public. While the movement gained global attention for the problem, some critics have labeled it "slactivism," since no specific outcomes resulted and the encampment had a distinctively "hippie" tone to it ('Pre-Occupied" n.a.) and the protesters were evicted from the park only two months later.

The Role of Public Relations

All three of these movements made extensive use of public relations strategies and tactics to advance their cause.

Huey Long reached the public by using his flamboyance and charisma. He was known to deliver dramatic speeches that garnered comparisons to church sermons. Long took advantage of the availability of the radio, and used it as a tool to communicate his ideals with the people. Long's radio speeches were very effective due partly to the fact that, by the 1930s, 90 percent of American families had a radio in their homes ("Radio's America" n.d.). Radio made it possible for Long to affect large groups of individuals in a far more intimate way than had been available before. And the popularity of newsreels was a great aid in building up (and even taking down) Long's reputation with the public.

Upton Sinclair used similar techniques to Long's in championing his idea. His election campaign also made use of special events, media coverage, and the distribution of flyers to take his message to the public.

Finally, the Occupy movement used social media to spread its message and gain supporters. A survey showed that 59 percent of its supporters engaged with the movement through Facebook and 70.6 percent through YouTube. The video for Occupy Wall Street was posted on YouTube about a month after the movement began ("YouTube," September 24, 2011). It features the encampment at Zucotti Park, which the demonstrators renamed Liberty Plaza, and shows individuals who had joined the movement in the park as they peacefully shared their views about changes they hoped to see as the result of their protests.

Internal communications also became critical to the Occupy movement as potential protestors formed a virtual community on social media to plan their activities before physically meeting at Zuccotti Park.

Conclusion

Long was assassinated in 1935. We will never know if he would have succeeded in implementing the plans he proposed in his "Share Our Wealth" program. But his presence was felt on the social and political landscape even after his death. Some have speculated that Long played a role in the shaping and emergence of FDR's New Deal (Amenta n.a.). As a result of Sinclair's EPIC campaign approximately 350,000 voters became Democrats in California. But his opponents waged a huge campaign, and Sinclair ultimately lost the gubernatorial race. While neither Long nor Sinclair fulfilled their ultimate political aspirations, they brought so much attention to their movements they have become part of the social and political landscape that informed the types of reforms that were made in America after the Great Depression.

Occupy Wall Street never resulted in any specific political or economic outcomes. But the protesters' efforts rekindled the debate about income quality in America.

Takeaway

This case shows that while communication channels tactics may have changed over the years—from newsreels and radio to TV and social media—the messages about income inequality still produce outrage and indignation. From the speeches of Huey Long to the footage of the "Occupiers," the topic continues to resonate with news reporters, op-ed writers, talk show producers and in this election year, even candidates for the presidency.

It was Senator Long who first brought the traditionally taboo topic onto center stage, where it was given due attention by radio and newsreels. But through the Depression, Second World War, post-war economic boom, and Vietnam, America's attention focused elsewhere. The issue lay relatively dormant for nearly 90 years. Not until the 2012 election cycle, (when a hidden mic recorded Mitt Romney's swipe at the "47 percent" of Americans relying on public support), did the issue spark the national front-page coverage it so deserved.

The media-savvy leaders of "Occupy," as it became popularly known, were experts at creating sound bites, visual effects, and rallying cries to attract reporters' attention. The idea of the "99 percent" has become embedded in our lingo today. And by keeping it on the front burner, the problem of income inequality has a chance of being rectified one day.

CHAPTER 13

Taking Depression out of the Closet

Depression has become widely recognized as a mental illness that can be discussed openly, treated with professional help and medication, and overcome. Sadly, this has not always been the case, and for some it remains a problem best left "in the closet." Thankfully, public relations campaigns designed to educate the public about depression are changing the picture for the better.

From Drills to Pills

Attempts to treat mental illness date back as early as 5000 BCE, as evidenced by the discovery of trepanned skulls in regions that were home to ancient world cultures (Restak 2000). Early man widely believed that mental illness was the result of supernatural phenomena such as spiritual or demonic possession, sorcery, the evil eye, or an angry deity, and so responded with equally mystical, and sometimes brutal, treatments. (Trepanning) first occurred in Neolithic times. During this procedure, a hole was chipped into the skull using crude stone instruments. It was believed that through this opening the evil spirit(s)—thought to be inhabiting one's head and causing their psychopathy—would be released and the individual would be cured (Holmes September 18, 2008).

In Ancient Greece, the physician Hippocrates believed that imbalanced body fluids, called humors, were the cause of mental illnesses and personality traits. The four humors—yellow bile, black bile, blood, and phlegm—were responsible for traits such as aggression, sadness, and empathy. In fact, the word "melancholy" comes from the Greek word for black bile, believed to cause feelings of sadness and withdrawal from the surrounding world ("Leo Sternbach's Obituary" 2005). For some, these symptoms were signs of genius; for others, depressive symptoms were signs of madness or illness.

The 18th to early 19th century was dubbed the "Age of Enlightenment." During this period, depression "was [seen as] an inherited, unchangeable weakness of temperament," and, unfortunately, because of this characterization, those who exhibited symptoms were shunned, became homeless and poor, and were committed to institutions (Foerschner 2010).

Electroshock therapy, now known as electroconvulsive therapy (ECT), was introduced in the United States in the 1940s. By passing electric currents through the brain, doctors were able to trigger changes in brain chemistry that can reverse the symptoms of some mental illnesses. It became used widely in extreme cases of depression. A study on its effectiveness was done by Dierckx, Heijnen, Broek, and Birkenghäger in 2012 that showed positive results in more than half the patients. ECT was brought to life for many Americans in Jack Nicholson's portrayal of R.P. McMurphy, an institutionalized mental health patient in *One Flew Over the Cuckoo's Nest*, the 1975 film based on the best-selling novel by Ken Kesey. In the film, Nicholson's character is subjected to repeated ECT sessions, and the procedure and the results are dramatically portrayed.

The 20th century also saw an increase in antianxiety and antidepression medications being sold to the public, dubbing it the "Age of Anxiety" (Henig 2012). The first of these, Valium, was introduced by pharmaceutical giant Hoffman-La Roche in 1963. It quickly became an enormously popular product. At its peak in 1978, the company sold 2.3 billion tablets ("Leo Sternbach's Obituary" 2005). Valium was marketed aggressively by Roche, using a wide range of public relations techniques, including publicity and product placements in films. For instance, in the movie *Starting Over*, Burt Reynolds' character has a panic attack in a department store and says "Does anyone have a Valium?" The punch line: every woman in the store reached into her purse and pulled out a little vial of pills (Henig 2012). Through Valium, Roche also pioneered advertising directly to consumers, a practice that was first allowed by the Food and Drug Administration (FDA) in the mid-1980s. The ads dramatized anxiety and depression in graphic ways designed to expose the pain caused by the illness and to offer relief to its victims.

Prozac, the commercial name for fluoxetine, developed by scientists from Eli Lilly, was approved by the FDA in 1987. Prozac quickly became the biggest-selling drug in the history of the pharmaceutical industry—a "blockbuster," the industry's equivalent to hitting a three-run homer out of the park (Eaton 2006). During the mid-1990s Prozac was one of best-selling drugs and was marketed as "the magic bullet" for people with depressive symptoms. "It was like bringing a meat cleaver down," says novelist Sarah Dunant, coeditor of an anthology of essays, *The Age of Anxiety*. She had a personal experience with antidepressants—saying they helped her through a tough time years ago. She believes Prozac has had far-reaching implications. "Things are not the same now as they were before," she says. Not everybody is happy about that (Nemade, Staats Reiss, and Dombeck 2007).

"What made Prozac good was not that it was potent, which it really was not, but that it had really good marketing," says David Healy, a professor at Cardiff University and the author of *Pharmageddon*. "They made us overcome the natural caution most of us have about pills and convince us that we absolutely had to have these things," Healy says. The marketing plan was subtle. Manufacturer Eli Lilly picked a name created by Interbrand that aimed to distance the drug "from everything typically associated with anti-depressants—strong chemicals, side effects" (McKelvey 2013). Prozac—as both a drug and a concept—caught on. Elizabeth Wurtzel's memoir *Prozac Nation* had a cult following. It was reissued in 2002, pegged to a movie starring Christina Ricci and sold more than 120,000 copies that year, according to *Publishers Weekly* (Eaton 2006).

Through books and movies, Prozac gave what critics claimed was chic gloss to a serious medical problem. After *Prozac Nation* was published, Wurtzel "went home with a different man every night and did heroin every day," she wrote recently in *New York* magazine (McKelvey 2013). The product enjoyed enormous media attention, even making the cover of *TIME* magazine.

Despite the often "glamorous" and "cool" portrayal of antidepressants in the media, depression itself still retained a stigma. Because of religious and cultural stigmas surrounding depression—often magnified by the media—sufferers find it very difficult to seek help. Not only does society still stigmatize the disorder, it looks negatively at those seeking help This has been found to greatly reduce the likelihood of depressives getting for help from a professional ("Harvard Case Study" n.a.). At times sufferers will even try to stop the pain of depression with more pain. Self-harm—including cutting, ingesting poisons, and even breaking bones—is inflicted secretly by depressed teens and young adults (McKelvey n.a.).

A common misconception about self-harm is that people are only doing it for attention. But more often than not they want to keep it a secret, keeping it away from parents, doctors, or mental health professionals. A common phrase is that they do it to "get out the hurt, anger, and pain" of their lives. Those who self-harm must get treated for both physical and mental pain, and the patient must be monitored for suicidal ideation (Jones 2015).

Depression, addiction, self-harm, anxiety, and suicide are more prevalent than ever. More than 120 million people worldwide suffer from depression—nearly 18 million people in America alone. Tragically, two-thirds of them do not seek help (Lawlor 2012).

With all the negative stereotypes, stigmas, and misinformation surrounding depression, more needs to be done to get "depression" out of the closet and onto the national agenda.

To Write Love on Her Arms

Fortunately, there are an increasing number of nonprofit organizations dedicated to doing just that. One is "To Write Love on Her Arms (TWLOHA)." The group's initial mission was raise funds to help bring professional support for a young person in need. Its mission today is to raise awareness for the prevalence of depression and its related activities of self-harm, eating disorders, drug addiction, and suicidal attempts.

In February 2006, a young man named Jamie Tworkowski wrote a story about his friend Renee Yohe. She had been struggling with drug addiction, depression, and self-harm and was trying to be admitted into a rehabilitation center. When Jamie met Renee, she was 19 years old. She felt that the world had already marked her for failure. To prove it, she carved the words "FUCK UP" with razor blades into the inside of her arm. She arrived at the rehab center the next day for treatment, but they turned her away, claiming she was too high a risk. For the next 5 days Jamie and his friends took care of Renee until they could find a different facility. To help pay for the treatment, Jamie and his friends launched a fund-raiser selling tee shirts with the words, "To write love on her arms." Thanks to the success of the fund-raiser, and the attention it brought for the issue, Jamie realized that an organization run by young people directed toward young people could well be beneficial to teens like Rene. And thus TWLOHA was born ("To Write Love on Her Arms" http://twloha.com).

In 2011 TWLOHA officially became a nonprofit organization. Its site describes its mission as follows:

1. To Write Love on Her Arms is a nonprofit movement dedicated to presenting hope and finding help for people struggling with depression, addiction, self-injury, and suicide. TWLOHA exists to encourage, inform, inspire, and invest directly into treatment and recovery (twloha.com).

From an Idea to a Movement

TWLOHA has become a depression awareness organization with an international following. To date it has responded to some 180,000 messages from young people from more than 100 countries around the world. Its founders have traveled more than a million miles to speak to community groups and meet personally with affected teens. It has hosted more than 600 blog posts of personal accounts from contributors around the world. Its fundraising activities have become so successful that it has been able to donate more than $1.5 million to treatment and recovery centers, and provided grants to nearly 75 unique researchers and counseling practices (twloha.com).

During the group's first tee shirt sale, the group's Myspace site began receiving messages from people who could personally relate to Renee's story. The group convinced famous rock bands, such as Switchfoot and Amberlin, to wear the shirts during performances. Plans are in the works now for a book and movie, all based on the struggles faced by teens like Renee. The organization has even helped universities open TWLOHA campus chapters. The organization also participates in the Vans Warped Tour—the largest traveling music festival in the United States (twloha.com).

Other Efforts

In the past 10 years, a growing number of nonprofit organizations have been set up to support those with clinical depression and anxiety disorder.

And thanks to the access and privacy afforded by the Internet, more young people than ever are comfortable seeking help ("Organizations That Offer Support With Depression and Anxiety" n.d.):

- *The Anxiety and Depression Association of America* (ADAA) website (www.adaa.org) offers a self-screening tool for individuals or their loved ones. It conducts grassroots campaigns to secure funding for research. It also holds "Mental Health Month" every May to draw attention to the issue.
- *Freedom from Fear* maintains a website that also offers self-screening tools. As with many of these organizations, its founder, Mary Guardino, was motivated to start the site following her own battles with depression. It created National Anxiety and Depression Awareness week in May, and offer educational and communications materials to support it.
- *The National Alliance on Mental Illness* (NAMI) is working to position mental illness as America's "last stigma." Its NAMI Walks Across America, now in its 13th year, has become the largest mental health awareness event in the country. Local organizers are provided with communications and organizational tools on the NAMI website (www.nami.org). The NAMI on Campus program addresses mental health issues "so that all students have a positive, successful, and fun college experience."

The Agenda for the Future

As much as these organizations are doing, however, more can be done. Public relations efforts prove that using personal stories and spreading information from credible medical sources can overcome the negative stereotypes, myths, and stigmas and help those suffering.

Takeaway

Mental illness, like many other social stigmas, has reached the national dialog in America through strategic communications campaigns. The once-hidden topic of discussion now gets addressed quite openly. Dozens of entertainers, politicians, athletes, and other famous people have opened up on the subject, and made it a widely covered topic in major media.

Personal experiences have often driven individuals to mount campaigns aimed at social change. Students Against Destructive Decisions (SADD) was founded by Robert Anastas, a high school coach whose students were killed in a drunk driving incident. Candace Lightner founded Mothers Against Drunk Driving (MADD) after her daughter was killed by a drunk driver. TWOLHA followed their excellent models.

Strong personal motivation enabled these individuals to fund-raise and attract professional support for solid strategic communications campaigns—often with dramatic results. They prove that while individualism remains strong in America, with the right messages and tools, the public can rally to support programs that promote the greater good.

CHAPTER 14

The Temperance Movement

America has a long, tumultuous, and drunken love affair with alcohol. It has been a part of the culture throughout the nation's history, but it has not always been a smooth relationship. Dating back to the time of the first settlements in America, boats carrying the pilgrims arrived stocked to the rim with beer, wine, and cider. In fact, these boats were possibly the first-ever "booze cruises" in American history ("West's Encyclopedia of American Law" n.d.).

At first, alcohol was looked at as a necessity because of its immunity to spoiling, but just a few decades later came to be seen as a societal vice. Alcoholic beverages have always had supporters and its detractors—creating an ongoing "bar brawl" that has spanned centuries.

Alcohol's biggest adversary came in the form of the Temperance Movement, considered one of the oldest social movements in America (Webb 1999). Beginning in the 19th and early 20th century, it was a masterfully organized, well-strategized public relations-driven effort that fought for the prohibition of alcohol as a way to improve American society.

Background

The Temperance Movement began to take shape in 1826. By then, America had gained an international reputation as the "alcoholic republic." And no wonder the average American male was drinking about 7.1 gallons of alcohol per year ("The Alcoholic Republic" 2003). This alarmingly high level of consumption caused many to begin looking toward the Temperance Movement for help.

Alcohol was portrayed by the movement as a form of slavery, with users helpless to its power. The movement positioned moderation as an invalid option, and advocated an all or nothing proposition (Murdach 2009). Members of the temperance movement wrote that

> . . . alcohol destroys the sense of decency and honor, silences conscience and deadens the best instincts of the human heart. [Furthermore, wherever] it touches human life it leaves the awful shadows of disease, crime, poverty, shame, wretchedness, and sorrow. (Murdach 2009)

The movement's members needed to develop a position which would, in their eyes, break the intoxicating shackles of alcohol. They argued that alcohol needed to be banned "to protect their neighborhoods, families and homes from the problems which are caused by alcohol" (Webb 1999).

The casting of alcohol as a national scourge soon began to impact the public psyche. The American Society for the Promotion of Temperance was created, which eventually came to be known as the American Temperance Society. The Society actively recruited members to strengthen its outreach efforts. They were able to turn a local initiative into a nationwide movement using innovative communication techniques. What started as a small organization soon spread and grew into thousands of smaller organizations across the United States. It eventually led to hundreds of thousands of individuals throughout the country fighting to ban alcohol ("How Stuff Works" n.d.). And it started to work. In the years between 1830 and 1840, consumption dropped by more than half. It marked the largest 10-year decrease in alcohol intake in American history (Bouchard 2011).

But this was only the beginning. A decade later, Maine voted to ban the manufacture and sale of alcohol—the first state to do so. This groundbreaking legislation was known as "the Maine law." Other states soon followed, though Maine would become regarded as the "birthplace of prohibition" ("Affordable Arcadia–Maine" n.d.). (It remained a dry state for 5 years after the end of national prohibition in 1934.)

States that followed Maine's lead and passed their own "Maine laws" were Delaware, Massachusetts, Rhode Island, Vermont, Connecticut, Indiana, Michigan, Texas, Ohio, New York, Pennsylvania, Iowa, and New Hampshire (Clubb 1856). Galvanizing public opinion in these states was considered the first step into full-blown federal prohibition. After a widespread communications campaign, the 18th Amendment to the U.S. Constitution was passed in 1920. It banned the sale, production, transportation, and consumption of alcohol anywhere in the country.

Prohibition was proof that the Temperance Movement's campaign had worked, eliminating legal alcohol in the United States.

The Public Relations Campaign

Passing an amendment to the U.S. Constitution is an arduous undertaking. It requires a two-thirds majority vote by both houses of Congress and ratification by 27 states. The feat took years of organization, word-of-mouth, promotion, church rallies, posters, public service advertisements, and full-scale demonstrations.

According to the Public Relations Society of America (PRSA), **"Public relations is a strategic communication process that builds mutually beneficial relationships between organizations and their publics."** It includes "planning and implementing the organization's efforts to influence or change public policy" ("Public Relations Society of America—What is Public Relations?" n.d.). Influencing and changing public policy was what the Temperance Movement was all about. It accomplished it a century before PRSA codified the approach. Contemporary public relations professionals use a wide range of tools to influence public opinion on social issues. Examples include campaigns like the Drive sober or get pulled over campaign, or Smokey the Bear's "Only you can prevent forest fires" (www.smokeybear.com/). These campaigns employ Public Service Advertisements (PSAs), "primarily designed to inform and educate rather than sell a product or service. The goal of a PSA is not to make a big sale, but rather to change public opinion and raise awareness for a problem." PSAs run on television and radio, and sometimes in print media as well (Suggett n.d.). Other elements used in issues management include social media outreach, publications, outreach to third party experts, editorial campaigns, and other communications techniques.

The Temperance Movement built its campaign using the tools that were available at the time. Radio and TV did not yet exist. So it spread its messages in other ways. The Movement employed a wide range of strategic messaging in its materials and advertisements. It raised sensitive subjects like the impact of alcohol on families, on one's health and, perhaps most strikingly, on one's masculinity. It associated excess drinking with immoral, "non-Christian" behavior. The movement started with logical and factual messaging, setting forth the dangers of drinking through printed materials like posters, books, pamphlets, and ads. Then it strategically added emotional appeals, positioning alcohol as an evil vice, and portraying anyone drinking it to be a less than respectable. Finally, it ignited public outcry against drinkers personally, using societal pressure to shame them.

Pamphlets and Promotional Materials

The world's first advertisements date at least back to the Ancient Egyptians in 2000 BC, carving out public advocacy messages in steel (Fox 2011). By the 19th century, the Temperance Movement leaders were able to do the same, but they had access to the greatest communications invention of all time: the printing press. Movement leaders created and distributed posters and pamphlets to reach townspeople wherever they were—in church, in the town square, or even in their homes. Messages took a dramatic tone, warning that alcohol leads to neglect of duty, moral degradation, and crime. Dramatic illustrations portrayed villainous alcoholics and the destruction they caused.

One particularly influential poster showed a mother and young boy with the big, bold appeal: "Please help me to keep him pure" (www.onbeyondz.net/cultural-change-womens-suffrage.html). By bringing mothers into the conversation, the message became personal and emotional, intended to make a reader feel guilty for favoring the bar over the mom.

The promotional posters did not always take a guilt-inducing approach. Some employed a scared-straight strategy. One showed an illustration of a young man going down a roller coaster, labeled the "Devil's Toboggan Slide," using illustrations from start to end indicating the predictable slippery slope of the alcoholic: "Popular Hotel or Drugstore, Saloons, Doggery, Gambling Hell, Corruption, and Drunkard's Graves." The final resting place of the "devil's toboggan slide" was a graveyard, invoking a religious claim against the vice (Clark 2015).

The movement also used messages designed to shame heavy drinkers in the hope that they would change their evil ways and, eventually, join the forces against the dangerous drinkers. The copy on another poster, in large headline type, yelled as follows:

> Hue and cry! Drunkard, you are a thief and a robber! You steal away your own respectability, your usefulness, and your integrity. You rob your family of their necessary means of support: You destroy their character for decency in their neighborhood, and you blast your children's future prospects in life. Drunkard, you are a public enemy! You bring a bad name upon working people generally, and shut up the hands of many who would do good to the poor, by showing before all men your base habits and brutal conduct (Temperance Movement, progressivespush4.wikispaces.com).

Media Relations

The Temperance Movement also used the power of the media and the credibility of many of its reporters to influence public opinion. They staged disruptive events that made local newspaper headlines. They penned op-eds and letters to the editor for inclusion in the dailies. They also wrote poetry and produced temperance-themed plays that drew the attention of reporters and spread the word about the dangers of alcohol. Some papers, like *The Progress* from Shreveport, Louisiana, dedicated regularly scheduled columns to the Temperance Movement ("The Progress" 1898).

The Temperance Union even published its own newspaper, the *Journal of the American Temperance Union*, devoted entirely to the temperance issue from 1837 to 1840. In addition, The National Temperance Society and Publishing House published numerous books and pamphlets about the sins of alcohol. Members wrote screenplays, like *The Drunkard* (Smith 1850), performed by actors before huge audiences at PT Barnum's American Museum in the 1850s (Burrows and Wallace 2000). Plays like this proved effective in reaching audiences where other types of media could not.

Rallies and Conventions

Rallies and conventions organized by the Temperance Movement created opportunities for like-minded individuals to converge and create new ways to influence public opinion. Because these were not limited to true "temperance" loyalists, the rallies attracted any curious individuals who may once have been on the fence. Every effort was made to convert these individuals into supporters.

Leaders staged rallies in churches, town halls, and many outdoor public spaces. An article from the *The Signal of Liberty* newspaper in Michigan described a temperance convention in Saratoga, New York: "The National Temperance Convention, held last week at Saratoga, was the largest ever held in this or any country. The number of enrolled members was 560" ("Signal of Liberty 1841"). These conventions and rallies were important because they proved to have a ripple effect, with word-of-mouth and follow-up articles. The movement also sent representatives to speak publicly in different parts of the country as ambassadors-at-large (encyclopedia.com 2013).

The national American Temperance Society was so successful that in 1832 it was able to join together some 2,200 temperance local groups throughout the country (encyclopedia.com 2013). With local "ambassadors" stationed across small towns in every corner of the country, speakers were able to take the "national" issue and localize it to make it more pertinent to the local communities. This is not unlike today's campaign to build local support for raising the national minimum wage to $15 an hour (Kasperkevic 2015).

Conclusion

Although Prohibition was eventually repealed, the Temperance Movement was successful in raising widespread awareness for the dangers of excess alcohol consumption, the message of which lasted well past the end of the Movement. It also laid the groundwork for future social movements and public health campaigns, such as those used to raise awareness for mental illness, driver safety, and smoking.

Takeaway

The Temperance Movement was important not only because of what was accomplished, but how it accomplished it. Limited communications tools were available in the mid-19th century. The period even preceded the invention of telephones and radio. Nonetheless, that which was employed—creation of advocacy posters, word-of-mouth campaigns, community rallies—were masterfully executed, and is still used in grassroots movements today.

The Temperance Movement was one of the first to seek changes to the Constitution in order to change society's behavior. So effective it was at building public support for its cause—especially among women—that Temperance laid the groundwork for nearly every other social movement that has followed.

Rarely in American history have we seen such a broad-based, long-term strategic communications effort achieving such an ambitious goal.

References

Chapter One

Virginia Shadron, "Popular Protest and Legal Authority in Post-World War II Georgia: Race, Class, and Gender Politics in the Rosa Lee Ingram Case" (Ph.D. Dissertation, Emory University, 1991), 30.

Charles H. Martin, "Race, Gender, and Southern Justice: The Rosa Lee Ingram Case," *American Journal of Legal History* 29 (July 1985): 251.

Gerald Horne, "Communist Front? The Civil Rights Congress, 1946–1956" (Rutherford: Fairleigh Dickenson University Press, 1988), 19.

Phillip Dray, "At the Hands of Persons Unknown: The Lynching of Black America" (New York: Modern Library, 2002), xi.

Eric W. Rise, "Race, Rape, and Radicalism: The Case of the Martinsville Seven, 1949–1951," *The Journal of Southern History* 58 (1992): 462.

Charles H. Martin, "The Civil Rights Congress and Southern Black Defendants," *Georgia Historical Quarterly* 71 (1987): 26.

"He Tried to Go With Me!" *Pittsburgh Courier* (March 20, 1948).

Untitled Document, CRC papers, Reel 5, Box 8.

Gerda Lerner, "Early Community Work of Black Club Women," *Journal of Negro History* 59 (1974): 158.

Erik S. McDuffie, "A "New Freedom Movement of Negro Women": Sojourning for Truth, Justice, and Human Rights during the Early Cold War," *Radical History Review* 101 (2008): 84.

"An Outline for Some Actions and General Program to Start Ingram Campaign," CRC papers, Reel 5, Box 8.

"Outline of Ingram Freedom Fight," CRC papers, Reel 5, Box 8.

"Petition to President Truman," CRC papers, Reel 5, Box 8.

"Statement of Mrs. Mary Church Terrell, Chairman National Committee to Free the Ingram Family," presented at the White House, Wednesday, June 1, 1949, CRC papers, Reel 5, Box 8.

"Voices From Abroad document", CRC papers, Reel 5, Box 8.

"Women Around World Protest Ingram Imprisonment," *Afro-American* (October 15, 1949).

"Mother's Day Card, 1950," CRC papers, Reel 5, Box 8.

"A Call to the Women of the United States," pamphlet, CRC papers, Reel 5, Box 8.

"Free Rosa Lee Ingram Fact Sheet," CRC papers, Reel 5, Box 8.

"Ingram Rally Invitation," CRC papers, Reel 5, Box 8.
"General Invitation Letter from Maude Katz," CRC papers, Reel 5, Box 8.
"The Facts of the Ingram Case pamphlet," CRC papers, Reel 5, Box 8.
"The United States Can Intervene for Human Rights flyer," CRC papers, Reel 5, Box 8.
"Statement from Emma Lazarus Federation of Jewish Women's Club for Conference and Holiday Season Prayer Meeting for the Freedom of Mrs. Rosa Lee Ingram and Her Sons in Atlanta, Georgia, on Friday, December 18, 1953," CRC papers, Reel 5, Box 8.
Jennie Truchtman, "Pilgrimage to Atlanta," *Jewish Life* (1954): 18.
"Family Finally Together Again: Now the Ingrams Have a Home," *Pittsburgh Courier* (June 25, 1960).
"Atlanta Nuptials: 'Blue Bloods' Attend Ingram Son's Rites," *Pittsburgh Courier* (September 10, 1960).
Rosalie Sanderson, "Mary Church Terrell: A Black Woman's Crusade for Justice" (Master's Thesis, University of Arkansas, 1973), 20.
Arlene Edwards, "Community Mothering: The Relationship Between Mothering and The Community Work of Black Women," *Journal of the Association for Research on Mothering* (2000): 89.
"Voices from Abroad Document," CRC papers, Reel 5, Box 8.
"Women Around World Protest Ingram Imprisonment," *Afro-American* (October 15, 1949).
"Ingram Plea Renewed: 50 Whites and Negroes Urge Georgia Women's Release," *The New York Times* (May 11, 1954).
"If You Would Be Free, Free Rosa Lee Ingram" flyer, CRC papers.
"Mrs. Ingram's 10 Children Miss Mother," *Afro-American* (February 25, 1950).
"Philadelphians Rally to Save Doomed Mother and 2 Sons," *Afro-American* (March 20, 1948).
"Statement from Emma Lazarus Federation of Jewish Women's Club for Conference and Holiday Season Prayer Meeting for the Freedom of Mrs. Rosa Lee Ingram and Her Sons in Atlanta, Georgia, on Friday, December 18, 1953," CRC papers, Reel 5, Box 8.

Chapter Two

Joseph Heath, "The Structure of Hip Consumerism," *Philosophy & Social Criticism* 27.6 (2001): 1–17. Web.
Atsuo Utaka, "Planned Obsolescence and Social Welfare," *The Journal of Business* 79.1 (2006): 137–148. JSTOR. Web.
Rick Tilman, "Thorstein Veblen and the Disinterest of Neoclassical Economists in Wasteful Consumption," *International Journal of Politics Culture and Society* 13.2 (1999): 207–223. JSTOR. Web.

John Chase, "The Role of Consumerism in American Architecture," *Journal of Architectural Education* 44.4 (1991): 211–224. JSTOR. Web.

Frank Trentmann, "Beyond Consumerism: New Historical Perspectives on Consumption," *Journal of Contemporary History* 39.3 (2004): 373–401. JSTOR. Web.

John Brewer and Roy Porter, "The Meaning of Consumer Behavior," *Consumption and the World of Goods* (Consumption & Culture in 17th & 18th Centuries series, New York: Routledge, 1994), 208. Print.

Peter Stearns, "Consumerism in World History. The Global Transformation of Desire," 2nd ed. (New York: Routledge, 2006). Print.

Nigel Whiteley, "Toward a Throw-Away Culture. Consumerism, 'Style Obsolescence' and Cultural Theory in the 1950s and 1960s," *Oxford Art Journal* 10.2 (1987): 3–27. JSTOR. Web.

Thorstein Veblen, "Chapter Four — Conspicuous Consumption," The Theory of the Leisure Class, *Kessinger LLC* (2010). http://www.gutenberg.org/files/833/833-h/833-h.htm.

Peter Stearns, "Stages of Consumerism: Recent Work on the Issues of Periodization," *The Journal of Modern History* 69.1 (1997): 102–117. JSTOR. Web.

"War Bonds for the War Effort," *The National WWII Museum*. N.p., n.d. Web. http://www.nationalww2museum.org/learn/education/for-students/ww2-history/take-a-closer-look/war-bonds.html.

"The U.S. Home Front at a Glance," *The National WWII Museum*. N.p., n.d. http://www.nationalww2museum.org/learn/education/for-students/ww2-history/at-a-glance/home-front.html.

"Women in WWII at a Glance," *The National WWII Museum*. N.p., n.d. Web. http://www.nationalww2museum.org/learn/education/for-students/ww2-history/at-a-glance/women-in-ww2.html.

"Victory Gardens during World War II". N.p., n.d. Web. http://www.livinghistoryfarm.org/farminginthe40s/crops_02.html.

"1940s War, Cold War and Consumerism," *Advertising Age* (March 28, 2005). Web. http://adage.com/article/75-years-of-ideas/1940s-war-cold-war-consumerism/102702/.

Adam Hart-Davis, "The American Dream," *History: From the Dawn of Civilization* (2015). N.p. Print.

Jessmyn Neuhaus, "The Way to a Man's Heart: Gender Roles, Domestic Ideology, and Cookbooks in the 1950s," *Journal of Social History* 32.3 (1999): 529–555. JSTOR. Web.

James Roark, Michael P. Johnson, Patricia Cline Cohen, Sarah Stage, Alan Lawson, and Susan M. Hartmann, "Understanding the American Promise," Volume 2: From 1865, *A Brief History of the United States*. (Boston: Bedford/St. Martin's, 2011). Web.

Andrea Ryan, "A Brief Postwar History of U.S. Consumer Finance," *Business History Review* 85.03 (2011): 461–498. U.S. Bureau of Labor Statistics. Web.

Jan Logemann, "Different Paths to Mass Consumption: Consumer Credit in the United States and West Germany during the 1950s and '60s," *Journal of Social History* 41.3 (2008): 525–559. JSTOR. Web.

Matthew Hilton, "Consumers and the State since the Second World War," *The ANNALS of the American Academy of Political and Social Science* 611.1 (2007): 66–81. JSTOR. Web.

Karen Brohl, "The 1950s: Pursuing The American Dream," *The News* (November 6, 2001). N.p. Web. http://www.achrnews.com/articles/87033-the-1950s-pursuing-the-american-dream.

"History: 1950s," *Advertising Age* (September 15, 2003). Web. http://adage.com/article/adage-encyclopedia/history-1950s/98701/.

Christine Zumello, "The 'Everything Card' and Consumer Credit in the United States in the 1960s," *Business History Review* 85.03 (2011): 551–575. Web.

Sandra Cain, "Key Concepts in Public Relations" (Basingstoke: Palgrave Macmillan, 2009). Web.

Scott Cutlip, "1987 Hall of Fame Award Acceptance Speech," *Arthur W. Page Society*. N.p., n.d. Web. http://www.awpagesociety.com/speeches/1987-hall-of-fame-award-acceptance-speech/.

Thomas Sowell, "Nader's Glitter," Insights. *Jewish World Review* (March 3, 2004). Web. http://www.jewishworldreview.com/cols/sowell030304.asp.

Max Brunk, "The Anatomy of Consumerism," *Journal of Advertising* 2.1 (1973): 9–46. Web.

Richard Buskirk and James T. Rothe, "Consumerism. An Interpretation," *Journal of Marketing* 34.4 (1970): 61–65. Web.

"1940s War, Cold War and Consumerism," *Advertising Age* (March 28, 2005). Web. http://adage.com/article/75-years-of-ideas/1940s-war-cold-war-consumerism/102702/.

"The American Dream of the 1940s & 1950s," *Ultra Swank* (October 9, 2013). N.p. Web. http://www.ultraswank.net/kitsch/american-dream-1940s-1950s.

"Television during the 1950s and 60s," *Living History Farm*. N.p., n.d. Web. http://www.livinghistoryfarm.org/farminginthe50s/life_17.html.

Kenneth Allan and Scott Coltrane, "Gender Displaying Television Commercials: A Comparative Study of Television Commercials in the 1950s and 1980s," *Sex Roles* 35.3–4 (1996): 185–203.

"Encyclopedia of Television—Soap Opera," *The Museum of Broadcast Communications*. n.d. Web. http://www.museum.tv/eotv/soapopera.htm.

"Misc 1950s Commercials (part 11)," *YouTube* (September 2, 2014). N.p. Web. https://www.youtube.com/watch?v=RR08gwRsyxY.

"1950's TV Ad Ford Car," *YouTube* (February 29, 2008). Web. https://www.youtube.com/watch?v=m7t9YlMxWoE.

"Folgers Coffee (1950s)—Classic TV Commercial," *YouTube* (July 29, 2012). N.p. Web. https://www.youtube.com/watch?v=RBBfqfOBbHw.

"1950s Laundry Detergent Commercial," *YouTube* (July 23, 2012). N.p. Web. https://www.youtube.com/watch?v=ChaRHzB2EpQ.

Robert Jacobson and Franco M. Nicosia, "Advertising and Public Policy: The Macroeconomic Effects of Advertising," *Journal of Marketing Research* 18.1 (1981): 29–38. Web.

William Young and Nancy K. Young, "The 1950s" (Westport, Connecticut: Greenwood, 2004). Print.

Don Bates, "'Mini-Me' History Public Relations from the Dawn of Civilization," *Institute for Public Relations* (2006). Web. http://www.instituteforpr.org/wp-content/uploads/MiniMe_HistoryOfPR1.pdf.

Edward Bernays, "Public Relations" (Norman: University of Oklahoma, 1952). Print.

Dan Schawbel, "10 New Findings About The Millennial Consumer," *Forbes Magazine* (January 20, 2015). Web. http://www.forbes.com/sites/danschawbel/2015/01/20/10-new-findings-about-the-millennial-consumer/.

Chrisine Barton, Lara Koslow, and Christine Beauchamp, "How Millennials are Changing the Face of Marketing Forever," *The Boston Consulting Group* (January 15, 2015). Web. https://www.bcgperspectives.com/content/articles/marketing_center_consumer_customer_insight_how_millennials_changing_marketing_forever/.

Patricia Parsons, "Ethics in Public Relations: A Guide to Best Practice" (London: Kogan Page, 2004). Web.

"What Is Strategic Philanthropy?" *Truist* (June 17, 2013). N.p. Web. http://truist.com/what-is-strategic-philanthropy/.

Jerry Marx, "Corporate Strategic Philanthropy: Implications for Social Work," *Social Work* 43.1 (1998): 34–41. JSTOR. Web.

Liv Kaufman, "P&G's Love Affair with Consumers," *Covalent Marketing*. N.p., n.d. Web. http://covalentmarketing.com/our-thinking/mkt_innov8/everyday-innovators/proctor-and-gamble/.

Jo Confino, "Procter & Gamble CEO on Solving the World's Sustainability Challenges," *The Guardian* (September 26, 2012). N.p. Web. http://www.theguardian.com/sustainable-business/procter-gamble-ceo-solving-worlds-sustainability-challenges.

"Dawn Saves Wildlife –You Can Make A Difference With Dawn," *Dawn Saves Wildlife*. Web. http://www.dawn-dish.com/us/dawn/savingwildlife.

"Companies in Action: Case Studies in Effective Corporate Disaster Relief," *Cone Communications* (August 30, 2013). Web. http://www.conecomm.com/case-studies-in-disaster-relief.

"About – Loads Of Hope," *Loads of Hope*. Web. http://tide.com/en-us/you-tide/tips-for-a-better-life/loads-of-hope.

Steve, "Causeaholic: Case Studies in Cause Marketing," *Causeaholic* (April 12, 2009). N.p. Web. http://www.causeaholic.com/2009/04/case-studies-in-cause-marketing.html.

"Chipotle," *Food with Integrity*. Web. https://chipotle.com/food-with-integrity.

Bettina Baylis, "How Chipotle's 'Food with Integrity' Strategy Can Really Succeed," *Triple Pundit People Planet Profit* (October 14, 2012). N.p. Web. http://www.triplepundit.com/2012/10/chipotle-food-with-integrity/.

Chapter Three

Earl Lewis, "Afro-American Adaptive Strategies: The Visiting Habits of Kith and Kin among Black Norfolkians during the First Great Migration," *Journal of Family History* 12.4 (1987): 407–420.

Joe Trotter, "The Great Migration in Historical Perspective: New Dimensions of Race, Class, and Gender," *Indiana University Press* 669 (1991): 8.

Janet Cornelius, "We Slipped and Learned to Read: Slave Accounts of the Literacy Process, 1830–1865," *Phylon* (1983): 171–186.

Ella Williams, "Harlem Renaissance," *AuthorHouse* (2010): 3.

Frances Steed Sellers, "The Ashes of the Father of the Harlem Renaissance are Finally Put to Rest in Congressional Cemetery," *The Washington Post* (September 12, 2014).

Cary Wintz, "Remembering the Harlem Renaissance" (New York: Routledge, 2013), 8.

Arnold Shaw, "The jazz Age: Popular Music in the 1920s," *Oxford University Press* (1989).

Chapter Four

Anna Brown, "As Congress Considers Action Again, 21% of LGBT Adults Say They Faced Workplace Discrimination," *Pew* (November 4, 2013). http://www.pewresearch.org/fact-tank/2013/11/04/as-congress-considers-action-again-21-of-lgbt-adults-say-they-faced-workplace-discrimination/.

Lou Chibbaro, Jr., "U.S. Professional Sports Called the 'Last Closet,'" *The Washington Blade* (August 28, 2013). http://www.washingtonblade.com/2013/08/28/u-s-professional-sports-called-the-last-closet-lgbt-sports-issue/.

Andrew Edwards, "Jason Collins Announcement: Other Athletes Have Come Out as Gay, but Only after Retiring," *Los Angeles Daily News* (April 29, 2013). http://www.dailynews.com/general-news/20130429/jason-collins-announcement-other-athletes-have-come-out-as-gay-but-only-after-retiring

"IU Expert on Sport and Masculinity Says Michael Sam Case Challenges 'Old School' Norms," *Indiana University*, press release, (February 11, 2014). http://news.indiana.edu/releases/iu/2014/02/michael-sam-jesse-steinfeldt-tip.shtml.

Chris Connelly, "Mizzou's Michael Sam Says He's Gay," *ESPN* (February 10, 2014). http://espn.go.com/espn/otl/story/_/id/10429030/michael-sam-missouri-tigers-says-gay.

"*Baehr v. Miike*," *Lambda Legal.* http://www.lambdalegal.org/in-court/cases/baehr-v-miike.

Richard Socarides, "Why Bill Clinton Signed the Defense of Marriage Act," *New Yorker* (March 8, 2013). http://www.newyorker.com/news/news-desk/why-bill-clinton-signed-the-defense-of-marriage-act.

"On Passage of the Bill (h.r. 3396)," *United States Senate* (September 10, 1996). http://www.senate.gov/legislative/LIS/roll_call_lists/roll_call_vote_cfm.cfm?congress=104&session=2&vote=00280.

"On Passage Defense of Marriage Act (h.r. 3396)," *United States House of Representatives* (July 12, 1996). http://clerk.house.gov/evs/1996/roll316.xml.

Anne Goldstein, "History, Homosexuality, and Political Values: Searching for the Hidden Determinants of *Bowers v. Hardwick*," *Yale Law Journal* 97.6 (1988): 1073–1103.

"Gay and Lesbian Rights," *Gallup*. http://www.gallup.com/poll/1651/gay-lesbian-rights.aspx.

Lawrence Tribe, "*Lawrence v. Texas*: The 'Fundamental Right' That Dare Not Speak Its Name," *Harvard Law Review* 117.6 (2004): 1893–1955.

"History and Timeline of the Freedom to Marry in the United States," *Freedom to Marry* (June 26, 2015). http://www.freedomtomarry.org/pages/history-and-timeline-of-marriage.

Obergefell v Hodges, 2015 WL 213646 (2015).

"Gay and Lesbian Rights," *Gallup*. http://www.gallup.com/poll/1651/gay-lesbian-rights.aspx.

Brinda Adhikari and Enjoli Francis, "Ellen DeGeneres Reflects on Coming-Out Episode, 15 Years Later," *ABC News* (May 4, 2012). http://abcnews.go.com/Entertainment/PersonOfWeek/ellen-degeneres-reflects-coming-episode-declaring-gay-15/story?id=16281248.

Bill Carter, "ABC is Cancelling 'Ellen,'" *The New York Times* (April 25, 1998).
http://www.nytimes.com/1998/04/25/arts/abc-is-canceling-ellen.html.

Kathleen Battles and Wendy Hilton-Morrow, "Gay Characters in Conventional Spaces: Will and Grace and the Situation Comedy Genre," *Critical Studies in Media Communication* 19.1 (2002): 87–105.

"This Day in History," *History*. http://www.history.com/this-day-in-history/coming-out-episode-of-ellen.

Nellie Andreeva, "'The Ellen DeGeneres Show' Renewed Through 2016–2017 Season," *Deadline* (March 11, 2013). http://deadline.com/2013/03/the-ellen-degeneres-show-renewed-through-2016-17-season-450595/.

Pat Griffin and Mathew Ouellett, "From Silence to Safety and Beyond: Historical Trends in Addressing Lesbian, Gay, Bisexual, Transgender Issues in K-12 Schools," *Equity & Excellence in Education* 36 (2003): 106–114.

"The Official Harvey Milk Biography," *Milk Foundation*. http://milkfoundation.org/about/harvey-milk-biography/.

Carla Crandall, "The Effects of Repealing Don't Ask Don't Tell: Is the Combat Exclusion the Next Casualty in the March Toward Integration?" *Georgetown Journal of Law and Policy* 10 (2012): 15–49.

Elisabeth Bumiller, "Obama Ends 'Don't Ask Don't Tell Policy,'" *The New York Times* (July 22, 2011). http://www.nytimes.com/2011/07/23/us/23military.html?_r=0.

"About," LGBT Sports Coalition, *Facebook Page*. https://www.facebook.com/lgbtsportscoalition/info?tab=page_info.

"Our Story," *Athlete Ally*. https://www.athleteally.org/about/.

"Our Cause," *The You Can Play Project*. http://youcanplayproject.org/pages/our-cause.

Cyd Zeigler, "By the End of 2015 There Will Be More Publicly out Athletes in Sport Than Actors in Hollywood," *Outsports* (January 7, 2015). http://www.outsports.com/2015/1/7/7508265/gay-lgbt-sports-entertainment-coming-out-2015.

H.A. Goodman, "Michael Sam Represents a Welcomed Evolution in America's Notion of Masculinity," *The Huffington Post* (May 27, 2014). http://www.huffingtonpost.com/h-a-goodman/michael-sam-represents-a-_b_5391235.html.

"The Role of Race in Jason Collins' Coming-Out Story," *Oprah's Next Chapter*. http://www.oprah.com/own-oprahs-next-chapter/The-Role-of-Race-in-Jason-Collins-Coming-Out-Story-Video_1.

Travis Waldron, "How Jason Collins Will Force Sports into a Leadership Role on LGBT Issues," *Think Progress* (February 24, 2014). http://thinkprogress.org/sports/2014/02/24/3322331/jason-collins-force-sports-leadership-role-lgbt-issues/.

Billy Witz, "Milestone for Gay Athletes as Rogers Plays for Galaxy," *The New York Times* (May 27, 2013). http://www.nytimes.com/2013/05/28/sports/soccer/milestone-for-gay-athletes-as-robbie-rogers-plays-for-galaxy.html.

ESPN.com News Services, "Jason Collins Says He's Gay," *ESPN* (April 30, 2013). http://espn.go.com/nba/story/_/id/9223657/jason-collins-first-openly-gay-active-player.

Ohm Youngmisuk, Ramona Shelburne, and Marc Stein, "Nets Sign Jason Collins," *ESPN* (February 24, 2014). http://espn.go.com/nba/story/_/id/10506550/jason-collins-sign-brooklyn-nets.

Dan Levy, "Robbie Rogers, Jason Collins & Gay Athletes: Plenty of History Still to Be Made," *Bleacher Report* (May 28, 2013). http://bleacherreport.com/articles/1653842-robbie-rogers-jason-collins-the-next-gay-athletes-share-a-place-in-history.

Cyd Zeigler, "The Eagle Has Landed: The Exclusive Behind-the-Scenes Story of How NFL Prospect Michael Sam Came Out," *Outsports* (February 9, 2014). http://www.outsports.com/2014/2/9/5396036/michael-sam-gay-football-player-missouri-nfl-draft.

John Branch, "Sam Says He's Gay: N.F.L. Prospect Michael Sam Proudly Says What Teammates Knew: He's Gay," *The New York Times* (February 9, 2014). http://www.nytimes.com/2014/02/10/sports/michael-sam-college-football-star-says-he-is-gay-ahead-of-nfl-draft.html.

Joe Drape, Steve Eder, and Billy Witz, "Before Growing Up, a Hard Time Growing Up," *The New York Times* (February 11, 2014). http://www.nytimes.com/2014/02/12/sports/football/for-nfl-prospect-michael-sam-upbringing-was-bigger-challenge-than-coming-out-as-gay.html.

Nina Mandell, "Missouri Students Black Westboro Baptist Church's Protest of Michael Sam," *USA Today* (February 15, 2014). http://ftw.usatoday.com/2014/02/missouri-students-block-westboro-baptist-churchs-protest-of-michael-sam.

Rebecca Shabad, "Lobbyist Drafts Bill to Ban Gays from NFL," *The Hill* (February 24, 2014). http://thehill.com/business-a-lobbying/business-a-lobbying/199057-lobbyist-drafting-bill-to-ban-gays-from-nfl.

Joseph Cabosky, "Queering Agenda Building: LGBT Advocacy Organizations and Strategic Information Flow Through Multiple Media Platforms" (Ph.D. Dissertation, University of North Carolina at Chapel Hill, 2015).

Rob Smith, "Jason Collins and Michael Sam Lead a New Era of Role Models for Black Gay Men," *Queerty* (March 6, 2014). http://www.queerty.com/jason-collins-and-michael-sam-lead-a-new-era-of-role-models-for-black-gay-men-20140306.

Ty Schalter, "Sam Says He's Gay: How Can Gay NFL Prospect Michael Sam Fit into Homophobic Locker-Room Culture?" *Bleacher Report* (February 15, 2014). http://bleacherreport.com/articles/1960845-how-can-gay-nfl-prospect-michael-sam-fit-into-homophobic-locker-room-culture.

Dan Hanzus, "Queering Agenda Building: CFL Players Fined for Negative Michael Sam Comments," *NFL.com* (February 11, 2014). http://www.nfl.com/news/story/0ap2000000325171/article/cfl-players-fined-for-negative-michael-sam-comments.

Chris Burke, "Donte Stallworth, Patrick Crayton Offer Differing Reactions to Michael Sam's Announcement," *Sports Illustrated* (February 10, 2014). http://www.si.com/nfl/audibles/2014/02/10/michael-sam-nfl-players-react.

Cavan Sieczkowski, "NFL's Jonathan Vilma Afraid Gay Teammate Would Look at Him in the Shower," *The Huffington Post* (February 5, 2014). http://www.huffingtonpost.com/2014/02/05/jonathan-vilma-gay-teammate-shower_n_4732415.html.

Peter King, "The NFL's Big Test," *Sports Illustrated* (February 9, 2014). http://mmqb.si.com/2014/02/09/michael-sam-monday-morning-quarterback.

TMZ Staff, "Michael Sam [video] Ripped Topless Dancing at Missouri Gay Club," *TMZ* (February 10, 2014). http://www.tmz.com/2014/02/10/michael-sam-topless-dancing-gay-bar-club/.

Aaron McQuade, "GLAAD Teams with Athlete Ally to Train NBA Rookie Camp," *GLAAD* (August 24, 2012). http://www.glaad.org/blog/glaad-teams-athlete-ally-train-nba-rookie-camp.

"Our Partners," *You Can Play Project*. http://youcanplayproject.org/pages/you-can-play-league-partners.

Seth Adam, "NFL Prospect Comes Out as Gay," *GLAAD* (February 9, 2014). http://www.glaad.org/blog/nfl-prospect-comes-out-gay.

Aaron McQuade, "NBA's Jason Collins Comes Out, Makes History," *GLAAD* (April 29, 2013). http://www.glaad.org/blog/nbas-jason-collins-comes-out-makes-history.

Renee Fabian, "Celebs Showing Support for LGBT Youth on #SpiritDay," *GLAAD* (October 17, 2013). http://www.glaad.org/blog/celebs-showing-support-lgbt-youth-spiritday.

GLAAD, press release, "GLAAD Calls on MLB, Atlanta Braves to Take Action After Atlanta Braves Coach Roger McDowell Uses Anti-Gay Slurs, Makes Violent Threats at Game," (April 27, 2011). http://www.glaad.org/releases/04272011braves.

Alexandra Bolles, "Wade Davis and Sarah Kate Ellis on Michael Sam and LGBT Athletes," *GLAAD* (February 12, 2014). http://www.glaad.org/blog/wade-davis-and-sarah-kate-ellis-michael-sam-and-lgbt-athletes.

Alexandra Bolles, "Snapshots: Michael Sam, Why Immigration Matters, LGBT Russians, and More," *GLAAD* (February 11, 2014). http://www.glaad.org/blog/snapshots-michael-sam-why-immigration-matters-lgbt-russians-and-more.

"GLAAD," *Twitter Page*. https://twitter.com/glaad?ref_src=twsrc%5Egoogle%7Ctwcamp%5Eserp%7Ctwgr%5Eauthor.

"GLAAD," *Facebook Page*. https://www.facebook.com/GLAAD.

"See Human Rights Campaign," *Facebook Page*. https://www.facebook.com/humanrightscampaign.

"Human Rights Campaign," *Twitter Page*. https://twitter.com/HRC?ref_src=twsrc%5Egoogle%7Ctwcamp%5Eserp%7Ctwgr%5Eauthor.

"Athlete Ally," *Facebook Post* (February 11, 2014). https://www.facebook.com/AthleteAlly/photos/pb.172220442802603.-2207520000.1442872249./733790886645553/?type=3&theater.

"See GLAAD," *Twitter* (February 12, 2014). 2:24 p.m. https://twitter.com/glaad/status/433728268509118465.

Cyd Zeigler, "Must Watch! Texas TV Commentator Dale Hansen on Celebrating Diversity & Michael Sam," *Outsports* (February 12, 2014). http://www.outsports.com/2014/2/12/5406580/dale-hansen-michael-sam

"GLAAD," *Twitter Post* (February 12, 2014) 2:24 p.m. https://twitter.com/glaad/status/433728268509118465.

"Human Rights Campaign," *Facebook* (February 13, 2014). https://www.facebook.com/humanrightscampaign/posts/10203061270590086.

Ellen DeGeneres, *Twitter Post* (February 12, 2014) 1:32 p.m. https://twitter.com/theellenshow/status/433715308356833280.

James Michael Nichols, "Dale Hansen, Pro-Gay Sports Anchor, Joins 'Ellen,'" *The Huffington Post* (February 14, 2014). http://www.huffingtonpost.com/2014/02/14/dalen-hansen-ellen_n_4790723.html.

"GLAAD," *Twitter Post* (February 10, 2014).

"Athlete Ally," *Twitter Post* (February 10, 2014).

"Athlete Ally," *Twitter Post* (February 19, 2014).

Brendon Ayanbadejo, "Opinion: Dungy has Selective Reasoning When it Comes to What is a Distraction," *Athlete Ally* (July 23, 2014). http://www.athleteally.org/news/opinion-dungy-has-selective-reasoning-when-it-comes-what-distraction/.

Connor Barwin, "My Job is Very, Very Different from Your Job," *Sports Illustrated* (February 28, 2014). http://mmqb.si.com/2014/02/28/connor-barwin-nfl-locker-room-culture.

Sean Gregory, "Be Smart, NFL: Football is Ready for Michael Sam," *Time Magazine* (February 11, 2014). http://keepingscore.blogs.time.com/2014/02/11/be-smart-nfl-football-is-ready-for-michael-sam/.

Wade Davis, "Interview by Author," *Telephone Call Tape Recording* (Chapel Hill, North Carolina, March 29, 2015).

Associated Press, "Gay Ex-Player Speaks at Meetings," *ESPN* (March 26, 2014). http://espn.go.com/nfl/story/_/id/10677444/ex-player-wade-davis-speaks-owners-meetings-gay-rights.

Nick Wagoner, "Wade Davis Addresses Rams on Sam," *ESPN* (May 16, 2014). http://espn.go.com/nfl/story/_/id/10933516/st-louis-rams-play-executive-address-team-michael-sam.

Lindsay Jones, "Owners Embrace Davis' Message on Respect for Gay Players," *USA Today* (March 25, 2014). http://www.usatoday.com/story/sports/nfl/2014/03/25/wade-davis-nfl-owners-meetings/6877715/.

Jeff Legwold, "Wade Davis Gets the NFL's Attention," *ESPN* (March 25, 2014). http://espn.go.com/blog/denver-broncos/post/_/id/5856/wade-davis-gets-the-nfls-attention.

Cyd Zeigler, "15-Year-Old Comes Out to Dad as Michael Sam is Drafted," *Outsports* (May 12, 2014). http://www.outsports.com/2014/5/12/5711208/michael-sam-son-comes-out-gay-draft.

Michael Lavers, "Sam Inspires College Athletes to Come Out," *The Washington Blade* (August 20, 2014). http://www.washingtonblade.com/2014/08/20/sam-inspires-college-athletes-come/.

Maureen Taylor, "Social Capital as a Measure of Public Relations Impact," *IPR* (February 10, 2011). http://www.instituteforpr.org/social-capital-as-a-measure-of-public-relations-impact/.

Chapter Five

International Movie Database (IMDB), "Thank You For Smoking Quotes." Web. http://imdb.to/1HbfTGk Accessed 15 April 2015.

Center for Disease Control (CDC), "Fast Facts About Smoking." Web. http://www.cdc.gov/tobacco/data_statistics/fact_sheets/fast_facts/. Accessed 15 April 2015.

Campaign for Tobacco Free Kids, "Toll of Tobacco in the U.S. Fact Sheet." Web. http://bit.ly/1GVF3si. Accessed 15 April 2015.

Center for Disease Control (CDC), "Fast Facts About Smoking." Web. http://www.cdc.gov/tobacco/data_statistics/fact_sheets/fast_facts/. Accessed 15 April 2015.

Xu, X et al., "Annual Healthcare Spending Attributable to Cigarette Smoking: An Update," *American Journal of Preventive medicine* (2014).

HHS, "The Health Consequences of Smoking – 50 Years of Progress A Report of the Surgeon General" (2014).

Public Relations Museum, "Videos of Edward Bernays Discussing Work for Lucky Strike Cigarettes to Attract a New Audience to Tobacco, the "Torches of Freedom" and the Green Ball Campaigns." Web. http://www.prmuseum.org/videos/?rq=luckystrike. Accessed 12 April 2015.

Office on Smoking and Health, National Center for Chronic Disease Prevention and Health Promotion, Centers for Disease Control and Prevention (CDC), "Achievements in Public Health, 1900–1999: Tobacco Use – United States, 1900–1999," *Morbidity and Mortality Weekly Report (MMWR)*. http://www.cdc.gov/mmwr/preview/mmwrhtml/mm4843a2.htm. Accessed 5 November 1999.

Respiratory Health Association, "50th Anniversary: Surgeon General's Report on Smoking." Web. http://www.lungchicago.org/tobacco-50th-anniversary-surgeon-general/. Accessed 12 April 2015.

Bradley, Diana and Laura Nichols, "Legacy Selects Ketchum as PR AOR to Boost Truth anti-smoking Campaign," *PR Week* (20 May 2014).

King James I of England, "A Counterblaste to Tobacco." www.laits.utexas.edu/poltheory/james/blaste.

Reducing Tobacco Use, "A Report of the Surgeon General," Chapter 2, (2014).

Ronald L. Numbers, "Prophetess of Health: A Study of Ellen G. White," *Wm. B. Eerdmans Publishing* (2008): 86

Matthew Hilton, "Smoking in British Popular Culture 1800–2000," *Manchester University Press* (September 2, 2000): 63.

Troyer, R.J., and Markle, G.E, "Cigarettes: The Battle over Smoking" (New Brunswick (NJ): Rutgers University Press, 1983).

"Achievements in Public Health, 1900–1999: Tobacco Use – United States, 1900–1999," *Morbidity and Mortality Weekly Report (MMWR).* http://www.cdc.gov/mmwr/preview/mmwrhtml/mm4843a2.htm. Accessed 5 November 1999.

"Surveillance for Selected Tobacco-Use Behaviors–United States, 1900–1994," *Morbidity and Mortality Weekly Report (MMWR).* http://www.cdc.gov/Mmwr/preview/mmwrhtml/00033881.htm. Accessed 18 November 1994.

Amos, Amanda and Margaretha Haglund, "From Social Taboo to 'Torch of Freedom': The Marketing of Cigarettes to Women," *British Medical Journal (BMJ)* 1.9 (2000). http://tobaccocontrol.bmj.com/content/9/1/3.full.

Bisbort, Alan, "Media Scandals in American History," *Greenwood Press* (2008): 37. https://books.google.co.in/books?id=3-4Yjb4C2JUC&pg=PA37&lpg=PA37&dq=bernays+%2B+surgeon+general&source=bl&ots=ibPf_rEj2J&sig=yMzCY_VzJR2JsJ-dYQOUxUzQLsg&hl=en&sa=X&ei=PDBJVfe_EfSAsQT2s4HYDw&sqi=2&redir_esc=y#v=onepage&q=bernays%20%2B%20surgeon%20general&f=false.

Blum, A, "Alton Ochsner, MD, 1896–1981 Anti-Smoking Pioneer," *The Ochsner Journal.* US National Library of Medicine National Institutes of Health, 1 (1999). http://www.ncbi.nlm.nih.gov/pmc/articles/PMC3145444/.

Curriden, M., "Inside the Tobacco Deal," *PBS Frontline* (1994). http://www.pbs.org/wgbh/pages/frontline/shows/settlement/timelines/fullindex.html.

Markel, Howard, "The Very Deadliest Habit. Book Review of Golden Holocaust," *New Republic* (March 29, 2012). http://www.newrepublic.com/book/review/robert-proctor-golden-holocaust-origins-cigarette-catastrophe-case-abolition.

"A Brief History of the Council for Tobacco Research," Originally Called the Tobacco Industry Research Committee Report (December 31, 1982): 21. Council for Tobacco Research Bates No. CTRMN039046/9066. http://bit.ly/1zaSG9T.

Kluger, Richard, "Ashes to Ashes: The Hundred Year Cigarette War, the Public Health and the Unabashed Triumph of Philip Morris," *Vintage Books* (1997).

"Harry Reasoner Anchors a CBS News Extra 'On Smoking and Health' Following the 1964 Release of the U.S. Surgeon General's Report Linking Smoking with Disease and Mortality," *CBS News Archives.* Web. http://www.cbsnews.com/videos/smoking-a-health-hazard-of-sufficient-importance/. Accessed 12 April 2014.

Center for the Study of Tobacco and Society, "Blowing Smoke: The Lost Legacy of the Surgeon General's Report" Online video clip, *YouTube* (Published on 8 January 2014). https://www.youtube.com/watch?v=M1zk5_xqOH4. Accessed 12 April 2015.

Elkayam, Alona, "Best/Worst Brands: Breaking Good, Afros and Crowdfunding," *Huffington Post* (26 April, 2013). http://www.huffingtonpost.com/entry/bestworst-brands-breaking-good-afros-crowdfunding_b_3158218.html?section=india.

Fox, Margalit, "Tony Schwartz, Father of 'Daisy Ad' for the Johnson Campaign, Dies at 84," *The New York Times* (17 June, 2008). http://www.nytimes.com/2008/06/17/business/media/17schwartz-tony.html?pagewanted=all&_r=1.

United States. General U.S. Surgeon, "The Health Consequences of Smoking: 50 Years of Progress. A Report of the Surgeon General" (2014). http://www.surgeongeneral.gov/library/reports/50-years-of-progress/sgr50-chap-2.pdf.

"Social Norms and Attitudes About Smoking 1991–2010," *Robert Wood Johnson Foundation, Center for Public Program Evaluation* (April 2011). http://bit.ly/1EZJcQS.

"Legacy Foundation Blog using Tobacco Atlas Stats." http://bit.ly/1FDd6u7 and http://bit.ly/1ErOmTT.

Tavernise, Sabrina, "E-Cigarette Use by Teenagers Soars, Even as Smoking Drops," *The New York Times*. http://www.nytimes.com/2015/04/17/health/use-of-e-cigarettes-rises-sharply-among-teenagers-report-says.html?emc=edit_na_20150416&nlid=37482102&_r=0. Accessed 16 April 2015.

Bradley, Diana and Laura Nichols, "Legacy Selects Ketchum as PR AOR to Boost Truth Anti-Tobacco Campaign," *PRWeek* (May 20, 2014). http://www.prweek.com/article/1296542/legacy-selects-ketchum-pr-aor-boost-truth-anti-smoking-campaign.

Morrison, Maureen, "Study: Millennial Parents Just Like Those From Previous Generations," *AdAge* (October 3, 2003). http://adage.com/article/news/millennials/244523/.

PM Horowitz, Class Lecture and Presentation, "The Millennial Effect How Gen Y is Changing the Way Business communicates," *Fall* (2014).

Chapter Six

U.S. Department of Health and Human Services, "The Health Consequences of Smoking – 50 Years of Progress: A Report of the Surgeon General" (Atlanta: U.S. Department of Health and Human Services, Centers for Disease Control and Prevention, National Center for Chronic Disease Prevention and Health Promotion, Office on Smoking and Health, 2014).

The Campaign for Tobacco-free Kids Fact Sheet, "Toll of Tobacco in the USA" (January 12, 2016).

The Campaign for Tobacco-free Kids Fact Sheet, "Toll of Tobacco Around the World". http://www.tobaccofreekids.org/facts_issues/toll_global/.

"New Survey: Indonesia Has Highest Male Smoking Rate in the World," *Campaign for Tobacco Free Kids* (September 12, 2012). Web. http://www.tobaccofreekids.org/tobacco_unfiltered/post/2012_09_12_indonesia. Accessed 21 April 2015.

Carriero, Rebecca, "Phone Interview with Mark Hurley" Conducted 27 April 2015.

"U.S Chamber of Commerce Works Globally to Fight Anti-Smoking Measures," *New York Times*. http://www.nytimes.com/2015/07/01/business/international/us-chamber-works-globally-to-fight-antismoking-measures.html?smprod=nytcore-iphone&smid=nytcore-iphone-share&_r=1

"CVS Health Leaves U.S. Chamber of Commerce over Smoking Stance," *The Wall Street Journal*, (July 7, 2015).

Chapter Seven

Best, Harry, "Reggae—The Music of Jamaica's 'Downtown' Masses," (1968–1981) *Oakland Post* (Alameda Publishing Corp. Ethnic News Watch, February 15, 1981), B13.Web. Accessed 23 April 2015.

Davis, Stephen and Peter Simon, "Reggae Bloodlines: In Search of the Music and Culture of Jamaica" (Garden City, New York: Anchor, 1977). Print.

Elias, Adam, "The Commercialization and Westernization of Rastafari and Reggae Music," *The Dread Library* (Debate Central—University of Vermont). Web. https://debate.uvm.edu/dreadlibrary/Elias.htm. Accessed 30 March 2015.

Jeans, Christopher, "Marcus Garvey Words Come to Pass: 1 A Black Revolutionary's Teachings Live on through Rastafarianism and Reggae Music," *The Dread Library* (Debate Central—University of Vermont, April 22, 1998). Web. https://debate.uvm.edu/dreadlibrary/jeans.html. Accessed 30 March 2015; Barrett, Leonard E, "The Rastafarians" (Boston, Massachusetts: Beacon Press, 1997) (66) cited in Jeans.

King, Stephen A., and P. Renee Foster, "Revolutionary Words: Reggae's Evolution from Protest to Mainstream," *The Routledge History of Social Protest in Popular Music*. Ed. Jonathan C. Friedman (New York: Routledge, 2013), 248–262. Print.

Nagashima, Yoshiko S, "Rastafarian Music in Contemporary Jamaica: A Study of Socioreligious Music of the Rastafarian Movement in Jamaica" (Tokyo: Institute for the Study of Languages and Cultures of Asia & Africa, 1984). Print; Smith, M. G., Augier, Roy, Nettleford, Rex, and University College of the West Indies (Mona, Jamaica), "The Rastafari movement in Kingston, Jamaica/by M.G. Smith, Roy Augier, Rex Nettleford," *Institute of Social and Economic Research, University College of the West Indies* [Kingston, Jamaica] 1975 cited in Nagashima (23).

"Rastas Mark 50th Anniversary of Bloody Coral Gardens Incident," *Jamaica Observer* (April 3, 2013). Web. http://www.jamaicaobserver.

com/news/Rastas-mark-50th-anniversary-of-bloody-Coral-Gardens-incident_13976856. Accessed 15 April 2015.

Spiker, D. Chad, "Reggae as Social Change: The Spread of Rastafarianism," *The Dread Library* (Debate Central'—University of Vermont, April 23, 1998). Web. https://debate.uvm.edu/dreadlibrary/spiker.html. Accessed 15 April 2015; Gayraud S. Wilmore, "Black Religion and Black Radicalism," *Monthly Review* 36.3 (July–August 1984): 121 cited in Spiker.

Lyrics from Desmond Dekker's Song "007 (Shanty Town)" from His 1969 Album *This is Desmond Dekker.*

duCille, Michel, "Black Moses, Red Scare; The Clash of Marcus Garvey and J. Edgar Hoover," *The Washington Post* (February 12, 1997): H 01 cited in Jeans.

Lyrics from "Don't Haffi Dread" by Jamaican Reggae Group Morgan Heritage.

Nikke Finke, "The Roots and the Practices of New Cult" *Los Angeles Times* (March 15, 1987): 1

Snippet from an article entitled: "Not Much Has Changed Since Coral Gardens Incident" from Jamaican Newspaper *The Gleaner* (April 7, 1963).

Chronixx, Interviewed by Lanre Bakare, "Chronixx puts Rastafarianism back into Jamaican Reggae: Dancehall's Brash Braggadocio isn't the Only Sound Coming Out of Kingston, Something that Diplo has been Quick to Cotton on to," *The Guardian*. Online Interview (October 11, 2013).

Martin, Tony, "Race first: the ideological and organizational struggles of Marcus Garvey and the Universal Negro Improvement Association," *The Majority Press* (1976): 10–14.

Chapter Eight

"Anti-Semitism: Alfred Dreyfus & 'The Affair'," *Jewish Virtual Library* (2015). https://www.jewishvirtuallibrary.org/jsource/anti-semitism/Dreyfus.html. Accessed 15 May 2015.

Beitler, Lorraine, "The Dreyfus Affair: Voices of Honor," *The United States Naval Academy* (2008): 1–47. http://www.usna.edu/Ethics/_files/documents/Dreyfusprogram.pdf. Accessed 13 May 2015.

Ben-Shalom, Reuven, "Hasbara, Public Diplomacy and Propaganda," *The Jerusalem Post* (June 12, 2014). http://www.jpost.com/Opinion. Accessed 15 May 2015.

"British Palestine Mandate: British White Papers," *Jewish Virtual Library* (2015). http://www.jewishvirtuallibrary.org/jsource/History/whitetoc.html. Accessed 4 May 2015.

Brustein, William, "Roots of Hate: Anti-Semitism in Europe Before the Holocaust," (Cambridge, United Kingdom: Cambridge University Press, 2003).

"Exodus 1947" (May 15, 2015). http://www.exodus1947.org/eindex.html

"Exodus 1947," *Holocaust Encyclopedia* (20 June 2014). United States Holocaust Memorial Museum. http://www.ushmm.org/wlc/en/article.php?ModuleId=10005419. Accessed 15 May 2015.

Friedman, Isaiah, "Theodor Herzl: Political Activity and Achievements," *Israel Studies* 9.3 (2004): 46–79. Academic Search Complete. http://web.a.ebscohost.com.remote.baruch.cuny.edu/. Accessed 5 May 2015.

Goodman, Giora, "'Palestine's Best': The Jewish Agency's Press Relations, 1946–1947," *Israel Studies* 16.3 (2011): 1–27. Academic Search Complete. http://web.a.ebscohost.com.remote.baruch.cuny.edu/. Accessed 5 May 2015.

Haron, Miriam Joyce, "Note: United States-British Collaboration on Illegal Immigration to Palestine, 1945–1947," *Jewish Social Studies* 42.2 (1980): 177–182. Academic Search Complete. http://web.a.ebscohost.com.remote.baruch.cuny.edu/. Accessed 5 May 2015.

McTague, John J, "Zionist-British Negotiations over the Draft Mandate for Palestine, 1920," *Jewish Social Studies* 42 (1980): 281–292. Academic Search Complete. Accessed 15 May 2015.

Miller, Rory, "The Rhetoric of Reaction': British Arabists, Jewish Refugees and the Palestine Question," *IsraelAffairs*14.3 (2008): 467–485. Academic Search Complete. Accessed 5 May 2015.

Morris, Benny, "1948: The First Arab-Israeli War" (New Haven, Connecticut: Yale University Press, 2008).

Nasrallah, Rami, "The Road to Partition," *Palestine-Israel Journal of Politics, & Culture* 9.4 (2002): 58–66. Academic Search Complete. http://web.a.ebscohost.com.remote.baruch.cuny.edu/. Accessed 5 May 2015.

Reich, Bernard, "A Brief History of Israel," 2nd ed. (New York: Checkmark, 2008).

Trescott, Jacqueline, "Holocaust Museum Remembers Exodus," *The Washington Post* (February 7, 2007). http://www.washingtonpost.com/wpdyn/content/article/2007/02/06/AR2007020601875.html Accessed 15 May 2015.

"War, Peace, & Politics: UN Partition Plan," *Stand for Israel.* http://www.ifcj.org/site/PageNavigator/sfi_about_war_partition. Accessed May 15 2015.

Zollman, Joellyn, "The Dreyfus Affair," *My Jewish Learning* (May 2012).

Herzl, Theodor, "Der Judenstaat," *Leipzig, M. Breitenstein's Verlags-Buchhandlung* (February 1896).

"British Palestine Mandate: British White Papers," *Jewish Virtual Library* (2015)
http://www.jewishvirtuallibrary.org/jsource/History/whitetoc.html. Accessed 4 May 2015.

Nasrallah, Rami, "The Road to Partition" *Palestine – Israel Journal of Politics, & Culture, 9.4* (2011): 58, Academic Search Complete, http://web.a.ebscohost.com.remote.baruch.cuny.edu/. Accessed 5 May 2015.

Chapter Nine

Friedan, B, "The Feminine Mystique" (WW Norton & Company, 1963).

Rottenberg, C, "The Rise of Neoliberal Feminism," *Cultural Studies* 28.3 (2014): 418–437. http://www.bgu.ac.il/~rottenbe/The%20rise%20of%20neoliberal%20feminism.pdf.

Sullivan, P, "Voice of Feminism's 'Second Wave,'" *The Washington Post* (2006): 5. http://www.washingtonpost.com/wp-dyn/content/article/2006/02/04/AR2006020401385.html.

Chapter Ten

Hanson, Ralph E, "Martin Luther King Jr., Civil Rights & Public Relations" (2012). http://www.ralphehanson.com/2012/01/16/martin-luther-king-jr-civil-rights-public-relations/. Accessed 7 April 2015.

Greene, Leonard, "How MLK's Right-Hand Man was 'Erased' from History," *The New York Post* (December 21, 2014). Retrieved from http://nypost.com/2014/12/21/how-mlks-right-hand-man-was-erased-from-history/. Accessed 7 April 2015.

King, Martin Luther, "Letter from Birmingham Jail," *The Atlantic Monthly* (August 1963).

"The Negro Is Your Brother" 212.2, (1963): 78–88.

Elliott, Osborn, "March on Washington," *Newsweek* 117.14 (1991): 10.

Fletcher, Michael and Reed, Ryan R., "An Oral History of the March on Washington," *Smithsonian Magazine* (July 2013). http://www.smithsonianmag.com/history/oral-history-march-washington-180953863/. Accessed 7 April 2015.

Bihm, J, "March on Washington," *Sentinel* (August 29, 2013): A.1.

"Testimony of John Lewis from a Hearing Resulting from the March 7, 1965, March from Selma to Montgomery in Support of Voting Rights," 295. http://www.archives.gov/exhibits/eyewitness/html.php?section=2. Accessed 7 April 2015.

The Seattle Times (2011). Retrieved from http://old.seattletimes.com/special/mlk/. Accessed 8 April 2015.

King, Martin Luther, "Letter from Birmingham Jail," *The Atlantic Monthly* (August 1963).

Chapter Eleven

Bao, Xiaolan, "Holding Up More Than Half the Sky: Chinese Women Garment Workers in New York City, 1948–92," *University of Illinois Press* (2001).

Drainville, André C, "A History of World Order and Resistance: The Making and Unmaking of Global Subjects," *Routledge* (2013).

Dworkin, Andrea, "Scapegoat: The Jews, Israel and Womens' Liberation," *Simon and Schuster* (2000).

Hood, Clifton, "722 Miles: The Building of the Subways and How They Transformed New York," *JHU Press* (2004).

Lederle, Cheryl, "Teaching With the Library of Congress" (March 18, 2014).http://www.laborarts.org/exhibits/thetrianglefire/2-the-clothing-industry.cfm.

Jensen, Robin E., Erin F. Doss, and Rebecca Ivic, "Photojournalism and the Pursuit of Social Justice," *Communication Currents* 6 (2011): 1–2.

Katz, Harry Charles, Sarosh Kuruvilla, and Lowell Turner, "Trade Unions and Collective Bargaining," *World Bank Publications* 1099 (1993).

Linder, Douglas, "The Triangle Shirtwaist Factory Fire Trial," available at SSRN 1024289 (2007).

Marrin, Albert, "Flesh and Blood So Cheap: The Triangle Fire and Its Legacy," *Knopf Books for Young Readers* (2011).

McEvoy, Arthur F, "The Triangle Shirtwaist Factory Fire of 1911: Social Change, Industrial Accidents, and the Evolution of Common Sense Causality," *Law & Social Inquiry* 20.2 (1995): 621–651.

Nancy L. Green, "Ready-to-wear and Ready-to-work: A Century of Industry and Immigrants in Paris and New York," *Duke University Press* (1997).

Odencrantz, Louise Christine, "Italian Women in Industry: A Study of Conditions in New York City," *Russell Sage Foundation* (1919).

Phillips, Charles, "March 25, 1911 Triangle Fire," *American History* 41.1 (April 2006): 16–70. "America: History & Life," EBSCOhost. Accessed27 May 2015.

Pool, Heather, "The Politics of Mourning: The Triangle Fire and Political Belonging," *Polity* 44.2 (2012): 182–211.

Russell-Ciardi, Maggie, and Education Director, "SUPPORTING MATERIALS."

Spitzer, Yannay, "Pogroms, Networks, and Migration" (2013).

Von Drehle, David, "Triangle: The Fire that Changed America," *Grove Press* (2004).

Weiss, Marc A, "Density and Intervention: New York's Planning Traditions" The Landscape of Modernity: New York City, 1900–1940 (1992): 46–75.

Yochelson, Bonnie and Daniel Czitrom, "Rediscovering Jacob Riis: Exposure Journalism and Photography in Turn-of-the-Century New York," *University of Chicago Press* (2014).

Young, Iris Marion, "Harvey's Complaint with Race and Gender Struggles: A Critical Response," *Antipode* 30.1 (1998): 36–42.

Burns, Ric and James Sanders, Lisa Ades, "New York: An Illustrated History," *Knopf* (1999).

Chapter Twelve

Amenta, Edwin, Kathleen Dunleavy, and Mary Bernstein, "Stolen Thunder? Huey Long's 'Share Our Wealth,' Political Mediation, and the Second New Deal," *American Sociological Review* (1994).

Cohen, Patricia, "One Company's New Minimum Wage: $70,000 a Year," *The New York Times* (April 13, 2015). Web. Accessed 29 May 2015.

"How Upton Sinclair and EPIC Swept the Democratic Primary 1934," *YouTube*. Web. Accessed 29 May 2015.

Lewis S. Ranieri, "Your Mortgage Was His Bond," *Bloomberg.com*. Web. Accessed 29 May 2015.

"Pre-Occupied—The New Yorker," *The New Yorker*. Web. Accessed 29 May 2015.

Radio's America, "Radio's America: The Great Depression and the Rise of Modern Mass Culture" by Bruce Lenthall, an Excerpt. Web. Accessed 29 May 2015.

"Tour the Project," Upton Sinclair's End Poverty in California Campaign. Web. Accessed 29 May 2015.

"U.S. Department of Labor—History—Americans in Depression and War." Web. 29

Wolff, Edward N, "Recent Trends in Household Wealth in the United States: Rising Debt and the Middle-Class Squeeze – An Update to 2007," *Levy Economics Institute Working Papers Series* (2010). http://papers.ssrn.com/sol3/papers.cfm?abstract_id=1585409.

Slote, Michael, "Moral Sentimentalism," *Oxford University Press* (2010).

Mitchell, Greg, "The Campaign of the Century," *Random House* (1992).

"A Message From Occupied Wall Street Day Five," *occupywallst.org* (September 25, 2011). Accessed 29 May, 2015.

"YouTube," (September 24, 2011). youtube.com/watch?v=5O_Ao9w1u7c.

Chapter Thirteen

Restak, Richard, "Fixing the Brain," *Mysteries of the Mind* (Washington, D.C.: National Geographic Society, 2000).

"Leo Sternbach's Obituary," *The Guardian* (Guardian Unlimited) (October, 2005). http://www.theguardian.com/society/2005/oct/03/health.guardianobituaries.

Allison Foerschner, "The History of Mental Illness," *Student Pulse Blog* (2010).

Robin Henig, *New York Times*, Sunday Review (September, 2012).

Clark Lawlor, "From Melancholia to Prozac: A History of Depression" (Oxford: Oxford University Press, 2012).

Rashmi Nemade, Natalie Staats Reiss, and Mark Dombeck, "Historical Understandings of Depression" (September 19, 2007).

Tara McKelvey, "How Prozac Entered the Lexicon," *BBC News Magazine* (April 10, 2013).

Margaret Eaton, "Harvard Case Study" (2006).

Audrey Jones, "Organizations That Offer Support with Depression and Anxiety" (2015). http://charity.lovetoknow.com/nonprofit-organizations-that-offer-support-people-depression-anxiety.

Jamie Tworkowski, "To Write Love on Her Arms" (2006). http://twloha.com/learn/story/.

Chapter Fourteen

"West's Encyclopedia of American Law," 2nd ed. http://legal-dictionary.thefreedictionary.com/Historical+Background+of+Alcohol+in+the+United+States.

Holland Webb, "Temperance Movements and Prohibition International Social Science Review" 74.1/2 (1999): 61–69.

"The Alcoholic Republic: Temperance in the United States," *The Journal of Presbyterian History (1997)* 81.1 (Spring 2003): 60–63.

Allison D. Murdach, "The Temperance Movement and Social Work," 54.1 (January 2009): 56–62.

How Stuff Works, "How Prohibition Works?" http://history.howstuffworks.com/historical-events/prohibition1.htm.

Kelly Bouchard, "Portland Press Herald" (October 2, 2011). http://www.pressherald.com/2011/10/02/when-maine-went-dry_2011-10-02/.

Affordable Arcadia, "Maine: First Dry State in 1851." http://www.affordableacadia.com/2010/maine-first-dry-state-in-1851/.

Henry Stephen Clubb, "The Maine Liquor Law: Its Origin, History, and Results, Including a Life of Hon. Neal Dow" (Published by Pub. for the Maine Law Statistical Society, by Fowler and Wells, 1856).

Public Relations Society of America, "What is Public Relations?" http://www.prsa.org/aboutprsa/publicrelationsdefined/#.VUkG__lVhHw.

Paul Suggett, "Public Service Advertising—A Complete Definition of Public Service Advertising." http://advertising.about.com/od/advertisingglossary/g/Public-Service-Advertising-A-Complete-Definition-Of-Public-Service-Advertising.htm.

Zoe Fox, "The Evolution of Advertising: From Stone Carving to the Old Spice Guy." http://mashable.com/2011/12/26/history-advertising/.

"The Progress" (Shreveport, Louisiana, December 3, 1898). http://chroniclingamerica.loc.gov/lccn/sn88064460/1898-12-03/ed-1/seq-7/.

"Journal of the American Temperance Union," 1–4 (1837–1840).

W.H. Smith, "The Drunkard; or, the Fallen Saved" (New York: WM. Taylor and Co.1850).

Burrows, Edwin G. and Wallace, Mike Gotham, "A History of New York City to 1898" *Oxford University Press*, 815 (2000). https://en.wikipedia.org/wiki/Edwin_G._Burrows.

"Signal of Liberty Newspaper" (September 1, 1841). http://signalofliberty.aadl.org/signalofliberty/SL_18410901 p3–15.

Encyclopedia, "Temperance Movements" (2013). http://www.encyclopedia.com/topic/temperance_movements.aspx.

Jana Kasperkevic, "Fight for $15: Workers across US Protest to Raise Minimum Wage—As it Happened," *The Guardian* (April 15, 2015). http://www.theguardian.com/us-news/live/2015/apr/15/fight-for-15-protest-workers-minimum-wage-live

Clark, George Faber, "History of the Temperance Reform in Massachusetts," *Forgotten Books, Classic Reprint Series* (June, 2015)

"Temperance Movement" progressivesapush4.wikispaces.com/Temperance+Movement\

About the Authors

Louis Capozzi has taught courses in business, consulting, and crisis management in the graduate programs in corporate communications at both New York University and Baruch College. He previously served as Chief Communications Officer of Aetna, and Chairman of the MSL Group, one of the world's largest public relations firms. A journalism and marketing graduate from the NYU Stern School of Business, he holds an MBA from Baruch.

Shelley Spector founded Spector and Associates 25 years ago, producing award-winning programs for clients like Embassy Suites, AT&T, Bayer, Philips, and ITT. She teaches the history of public relations in the graduate program in corporate communications at Baruch, and is also founder of the world's first Museum of Public Relations. A journalism graduate of the University of Rhode Island, she holds an MS in Radio/Television from the Newhouse School at Syracuse University.

Index

OTHER TITLES IN OUR PUBLIC RELATIONS COLLECTION

Don W. Stacks and Donald K. Wright, *Editors*

- *A Professional and Practitioner's Guide to Public Relations Research, Measurement, and Evaluation, Second Edition* by David Michaelson and Donald W. Stacks
- *Leadership Communication: How Leaders Communicate and How Communicators Lead in Today's Global Enterprise* by E. Bruce Harrison and Judith Muhlberg
- *The Public Relations Firm* by Stacey Smith and Bob Pritchard
- *Public Relations Ethics: How To Practice PR Without Losing Your Soul* by Dick Martin and Donald K. Wright
- *MetricsMan: It Doesn't Count Unless You Can Count It* by Don Bartholomew and Zifei Fay Chen

Business Expert Press has over 30 collection in business subjects such as finance, marketing strategy, sustainability, public relations, economics, accounting, corporate communications, and many others. For more information about all our collections, please visit www.businessexpertpress.com/collections.

Business Expert Press is actively seeking collection editors as well as authors. For more information about becoming an BEP author or collection editor, please visit http://www.businessexpertpress.com/author

Announcing the Business Expert Press Digital Library

Concise e-books business students need for classroom and research

This book can also be purchased in an e-book collection by your library as

- *a one-time purchase,*
- *that is owned forever,*
- *allows for simultaneous readers,*
- *has no restrictions on printing, and*
- *can be downloaded as PDFs from within the library community.*

Our digital library collections are a great solution to beat the rising cost of textbooks. E-books can be loaded into their course management systems or onto students' e-book readers. The **Business Expert Press** digital libraries are very affordable, with no obligation to buy in future years. For more information, please visit **www.businessexpertpress.com/librarians.** To set up a trial in the United States, please email **sales@businessexpertpress.com.**

Printed in the USA
CPSIA information can be obtained
at www.ICGtesting.com
CBHW080005150224
4365CB00009B/642